# ENDORSEMENTS

"First of all, I know that all of you will enjoy getting to know Alane Haynes as an author. I love the way Alane writes and continues to help the reader become one with what she is writing. Alane is a Godly woman of faith who is aligned apostolically in the region. Because of this, she has a peculiar unction to establish truth.

Prepare to be illuminated in the revelation that God is releasing and get ready to be challenged as you read this enlightening book. Alane has meticulously given to the reader an ability to learn and to absorb God's ways. She understands oneness with the Godhead and endeavors to keep the unity of the Spirit in the bond of peace.

Shocked... will jolt you to think, and to allow the Lord to calibrate His mindset into your belief system. You have been given the mind of Christ and Alane confronts the reader to assess this truth by identifying where they are and where they need to be as part of this great end-time army of the Lord."

—Apostle Billie Alexander
Co-Founder and President
Limitless Realms Int'l Ministries
Greater San Diego Region

"There are several types of writers tapping their keyboards these days. Some use mere words to paint their black and white pictures. Contrarily, I have found Alane Haynes to be a writer of thought-provoking images. Her book entitled "Shocked" is as electrifying as her title. Her unique perspective on Biblical truths is a pleasing eye-opener. If you hunger for compelling perspectives on God's Word, I think you will enjoy this."

—Caz Taylor
Bible Teacher and Author

# Moses-Shocked in the Desert

# MOSES-SHOCKED IN THE DESERT

*Learning God's Ways So We Can Enter the Promised Land*

ALANE HAYNES

**TATE PUBLISHING**
AND **ENTERPRISES**, LLC

Published by Tate Publishing & Enterprises, LLC
127 E. Trade Center Terrace | Mustang, Oklahoma 73064 USA
1.888.361.9473 | www.tatepublishing.com

Tate Publishing is committed to excellence in the publishing industry. The company reflects the philosophy established by the founders, based on Psalm 68:11,
*"The Lord gave the word and great was the company of those who published it."*

Book design copyright © 2014 by Tate Publishing, LLC. All rights reserved.
*Cover design by Rodrigo Adolfo*
*Interior design by Joana Quilantang*

Published in the United States of America

ISBN: 978-1-63063-907-5
1. Religion / Christian Life / Personal Growth
2. Religion / Christian Life / Spiritual Growth
14.02.24

# CONTENTS

# PREFACE

What I am going to say here may be shocking to some, which is appropriate since the book itself provides examples of God sometimes shocking us to get us into the place and/or position He wants us. I think God wants me to tell you how He told me to write this book. It was not an audible voice. It was not an impression. It was through a series of events that led me to the conclusion and then other events confirming.

My writing background up to that point had been creative writing in high school, writing reports at work, taking a course in writing children's books, journaling, and, most directly related, writing poems. The poems were birthed out of inspiration from scripture; as I studied His Word, my spirit inside me was overwhelmed with revelation of God, Jesus Christ, and the Holy Spirit and the poems flowed. Over the course of a few years, I wrote approximately two hundred and felt I should try and publish them. I submitted them to a number of publishers and most wrote that, although they were good, it wasn't what they were looking to publish. I was very discouraged for some time, then came to the conclusion that perhaps the poems were really just for me, to build my faith. I had a desire to write for a living but had not pursued it other than the coursework. My career had been largely administrative up to that point.

Fast-forward about ten years, at the beginning of the New Year. I had been ill with stomach flu so had not eaten anything for about three days (a fast I hadn't chosen). I had a very odd dream. I dreamt that I was in a large room full of people that, over the years, had a great impact on my life spiritually. I was talking to one woman who, in real life, had only been married one year, worked full-time, and just had a baby. She told me that she had written a book. I was surprised and interested, and asked her the title. She said, "Moses—Shocked in the Desert." I was intrigued, then kind of angry. I said, "How do you have time to write? I feel like I'm supposed to write, and I don't know how you could have time to write when you have a young baby and work full-time."

Then I woke up. It was about 2:00 a.m., and I had a blinding migraine. I was lying there, trying to go back to sleep so that I wouldn't feel the migraine, but I kept thinking about the dream and wondering about the meaning, because the dream had been so vivid and seemed to be potent with meaning. As I lay there, I thought, What? God, are you telling me you want me to write a book and that is the title? Immediately, I felt the Holy Spirit impressing scripture upon me. I got up and stumbled into the den, turned on the light, and began writing down the scriptures I heard (with difficulty focusing because the light was blinding me from the migraine). After I wrote them down, I felt release and went back to bed and was able to go back to sleep.

The next two nights the same thing happened—waking up at 2:00 a.m. with scriptures jumping in my spirit, and a migraine. The third night, I said to God, "Okay, I get it. I'll get up when you wake me, but how about no more headaches." Thankfully, over the course of the writing of the book, when I was awakened with scriptures jumping, there was not a migraine accompanying them. I also told God that this time, it had to be all Him; in other words, I would write it, but I wasn't going to try and make something happen afterward; it had to be fully led by Him.

Also around this time, I went to my favorite devotional (that I hadn't looked at when I was ill) and looked up the reading for the morning after the dream. It said, "Write what I tell you." I am not kidding. You can imagine my reaction. I was stunned and amazed. Another confirmation of this being God was that the next week I was having lunch with a friend who moves in the prophetic, and as I was sharing what had happened, she asked me, "When you had the migraines, what side of your head was the pain on?" I said, "The right." She then asked me, "What does that represent?" I said, "Creativity," and just about fell out of my chair at the significance.

Over the next few years, when I would become discouraged and begin to doubt whether God really wanted me to write this book, He would immediately bring additional scriptures and inspiration to me. After I spent about a year or so editing what I had written and trying to get it into some kind of order (which was grueling), I had to put it down for a while.

God divinely arranged relationships with key people who would speak a prophetic word to me about writing at pivotal moments. He arranged circumstances aligning me with a writer/ writing instructor at a church we were both attending whose class I was able to attend. Our paths separated for a time, and recently God brought us back together again in His perfect timing and positioning. I was contemplating submitting the book to some publishing companies when this realignment took place and my friend said he would take a look at the book.

So that is how I came to believe that this is a book God wanted written. His ways are not our ways; that is for sure!

# INTRODUCTION

There are times when we go through life completely unaware of God. We believe but do not see or hear. Our spiritual senses are dulled, perhaps because our natural senses have been oversaturated. We become oversaturated in part by the fast-paced tempo of the material world, in part because we fill our lives with things that bring us satisfaction on a temporal level. Or our spiritual senses may have become dulled by our disobedience to His voice, as we chose to listen to and follow our own voice or other voices. God will allow us to be dulled, giving us our heart's desires, so that we can see what life is like when we follow our own desires. He knows that we will become dissatisfied, because we were created with a void in our hearts that only He can fill. He created us with a purpose, and nothing else will satisfy. Thankfully, He will only allow us to go so far before He will intervene with His "shock treatment." He will also do this when we have become complacent and He wants to bring us to greater revelation of who He is so that He can bring us to greater responsibility and authority in accordance with His purpose for our lives. He is always looking out for our good to fulfill His purpose in our lives. My prayer is that through the examples in this book, the Holy Spirit will show you, as He did me, things that will "shock you awake" spiritually; that He will open your eyes to another perspective, a dimension that you may not be aware of, or have forgotten momentarily; and that He will be revealed to you in a new way. I pray that this scripture will take on greater meaning in your life: "The people that walk in darkness have seen a great light" (Matt. 4:16; Isa. 9:2). Further, I pray that you go forward encouraged to search Him out as hidden treasure in every circumstance in your life and, finding Him, glorify His name.

As the Holy Spirit brings revelation to your life, be aware that it may not look like you think it should—you may be shocked. This is good! Like the shock of cold water when you are lulled into laziness by the warmth of the sun and the sound of the waves; after your body is shocked, your senses are alert again.

As you seek to apply what the Holy Spirit shows you, you may feel loss and resistance. Perhaps this will manifest as loss of an ungodly belief system or loss of an aspect of your identity that does not line up with who God created you to be. The ego will fight to maintain its identity. You may feel insecurity and fear when you are shocked to the reality that there are things outside your control. We don't like that. We spend most of our lives trying to create a sense of security around us. We create caves of darkness that are comfortable to us. Our sight adjusts to the darkness. Be prepared. A man living in a cave is blinded by the light when he first comes out, and can see nothing at first, then only dim images. Conversely, a person sitting in the bright summer sun all day long, when walking into a darkened movie theater, can see nothing. There will be a transition period as you adjust to the light of the truth, trying to fit it into your belief system—something will have to go; trust me, God has His ways to convert you into His way of thinking.

As you are shocked awake, you will begin to look at life a little differently, more in tune with His Spirit, so that you can better see, hear, and sense what God is saying and doing.

When you are shocked by His revelation to you of His ways versus your ways, and His thoughts versus your thoughts, wait on the Holy Spirit and allow Him to reveal to you the heart of Jesus in the intimate details of your life. His knowledge of you will rightly position your mind to His sovereignty, and His love for you will provide the grace needed to move in the direction of His purpose for your life.

I hear Him saying, "Incline your ear, and come unto me: hear, and your soul shall live; and I will make an everlasting covenant with you, even the sure mercies of David" (Isaiah 55:3). Obviously, we are already living, so what does He mean? There is a greater place, a deeper place, a higher place, a wider place, where we are more aware of the spiritual realm (invisible to the natural senses) where He is. There is a great freedom in this place, as your awareness of God increases, where you are alert and awake, spiritually; a place where your spiritual eyes can see and your spiritual ears can hear; a place where you are one with Him, walking in the restoration of Father/child relationship that Jesus paid the price for.

We recognize the process of maturity is learning from what happened—if this, then that…seeing consequences of our actions and words. We understand that if we touch a hot oven we get burned. We learn that if we yell at the people around us they leave and we are alone. We learn that if we overindulge, our bodies react.

Yet most of the time we aren't paying attention spiritually—we waste a lot of time and find ourselves in the same situation over and over. The players and scenes may change, but there is a sense of déjà vu, or awareness that we keep experiencing the same things in our lives. Why? We aren't listening, seeing, or sensing. God is giving us opportunities in the classroom of the Spirit, but we don't have a clue. If we don't pay attention and continue to just react by our feelings, we begin to operate from a victim mentality or trying to control everything and everyone. God is trying to get us to turn to Him. He has a way out. He has a plan.

We can learn a lot from the experiences of the Israelites, who took forty years to finish an eleven-day journey, and most of them didn't even get to enter in to the Promised Land, including Moses, the leader. All along, God wanted to be their God. He told them if they would listen and obey, they would be blessed (Deut. 28). It seems so simple. What happened? We can learn from the examples of the Israelites and others in the Bible by applying it to our own lives. If our eyes are opened to God's ways, we can better understand what He is doing. If we begin to look for Him in everything, we will be in a better position to fulfill our God-given destiny. As we learn His ways, we get a better understanding of who He is, and when we know Him, it is easier to obey. We learn that He is completely trustworthy, that He loves us and created us for a purpose. We read in Daniel 11:32, "A people that know their God will do mighty exploits." God wants us to be restored to that relationship that was intended from the beginning. One way He makes Himself known is by supernatural acts. Our role, as Christians, is to allow the Holy Spirit to move through us so that others will come to Him, an example shown us in the life of Christ. We read in Acts 10:38 that "Jesus went about doing good and healing all who were oppressed of the devil." He sent the disciples—first the twelve, then seventy, then commissioned all of us to do the same (Luke 9:1–6, 10:1–20; Mark 16:15–20; John 14:12–14, 20:19–21).

When you have a job, it is vital to listen closely and do exactly what you are told to do—no more, no less. When God speaks to us, it is the precision that is imperative in many cases. The one little thing left out seemingly insignificant to us, yet not to God. There is nothing insignificant in any of His words or actions. What is faith, after all, if not belief in what someone has said to the point of taking corresponding action? You have faith in electricity, so you flip the switch to turn on the light. You have faith in gravity, so you don't walk off a mountaintop. You have faith that your employer will pay you as they said they would, so you show up every day and follow their instructions.

Examples given in this book will show that God will shock us out of our complacency and spiritual blindness to the reality that He has given us creative power…what are we creating? We create atmospheres and situations by our words. In James 3:1–10, we read that our tongue is like the rudder of a ship and that it sets in motion the course of our lives.

From Sinai (where they received holiness instructions) to Kadesh-Barnea, the people were wandering. The wilderness was part of necessary discipleship, for growth in relationship with God, but wandering was due to their complaining and unbelief. There is a difference between wilderness and wandering. Jesus was sent into the wilderness, but He never wandered aimlessly. Even though God had shown the Israelites His love and faithfulness, in delivering them from Egypt, they did not believe in their heart of hearts that He was good. Why? What is it in us that refuses to believe God is good?

- We want what we want when we want it, and like spoiled children, if we don't get it, we think God is holding out or the enemy is hindering us.

- We think that we are not worthy; in our heart of hearts we believe we deserve punishment; we don't deserve His goodness. Yet rather than confess our sin and stay in that place of humility, our flesh still wants to be our own god and relieve our momentary afflictions.

- We are deceived by the world, flesh or the devil to think that we should control our own destiny, and we may even rationalize by thinking that our thoughts are God's thoughts, deceiving ourselves even further as we justify our beliefs by misapplying scripture to our situation.

Let us never forget this was Satan's ploy as he tempted Christ in the wilderness. In Luke we can read Satan's temptation and Jesus's response, "If thou be the Son of God, cast thyself down from hence: For it is written, He shall give his angels charge over thee, to keep thee: And in their hands they shall bear thee up, lest at any time thou dash thy foot against a stone. Jesus answering said unto him, It is said, Thou shalt not tempt the Lord thy God" (Luke 4:9–12 KJV). Satan left out an important part when he quoted scripture. He omitted, "He that dwelleth in the secret place of the most High shall abide under the shadow of the Almighty. I will say of the Lord, He is my refuge and my fortress: my God; in him will I trust" (Ps. 91:1–2 KJV). Jesus knew that the only safe place of refuge is in the perfect will of God, regardless of how it looks to us in the natural.

We often place ourselves in situations God never told us to go into, yet we claim His blessing upon it. Thank God for His mercy in rescuing us when we come to our senses and realize that we need Him desperately, and that His way is the right way.

Earlier, a different twist on this was when Satan got Eve to doubt what God said (Gen. 3:1) then implied that God had evil motives (Gen. 3:4–5). Therein lies the apple awaiting all of us—do we trust that God is good? Do we even believe what God has said? Do we even know what He said? Do we even believe He speaks? Do we think our thoughts are His thoughts? Do we pay attention to our thoughts long enough to try and discern whose thoughts they are or what impact they have on our lives? If we don't pay attention to our thoughts and discern correctly where they originate, we will never move forward; we will continually be going around the mountains that we face.

You may be surprised to find that there is a purpose to the trial. You may be more surprised when you find that you hold the key to the end of it. It is easy and pacifying to say "God is in control" and "I'm just trusting God" and doing nothing. After reading this book, you may find that, yes, God is in control, but He is waiting for you to listen to what He is saying in your circumstances, to see what He is doing and respond correctly.

I hope and pray that by the time you have finished reading this book, you will be better able to recognize His voice, your own thoughts, the voice of the world and the enemy. Also, that you will be better positioned and equipped to move forward into your God-given destiny, through revelation of who He is and recognition of His ways in your life. Let God speak to you through the biblical examples, the Holy Spirit showing you how they apply to your life today, and move through the desert/wilderness into the land He has promised to you. In 1 Corinthians 10:6–13, Paul exhorts us to recognize that the account of the Israelite's experience was written as an example for us so that we would not fall as they did.

# SHOCKING: THE REALITY THAT GOD IS, AND HE DESIRES A RELATIONSHIP WITH US

## Shocking: God Has Always Desired Communion with Man

### ADAM

In the beginning, God created the heavens and the earth. He created man in His image so that He could have relationship. He walked with Adam and Eve in the cool of the garden, seeking them out. Their relationship was simple and pure, until they sinned. Then they hid. God still sought them out. Finding them, He wanted to continue in relationship though they had sinned. He immediately began the process of restoration, covering them with robes made of blood sacrifice. In order for continued fellowship with God, there had to be the shedding of blood for remission of sins. Animal sacrifice in the Old Testament was a precursor to Jesus's ultimate atonement, yet there was much to learn before that was to take place. We had to learn the true nature of sin and its destructive power so that we could appreciate fully and embrace with humility our role in relationship with God, the reality that we are dependent upon Him. There is no good thing in us, in our human nature, because our hearts are selfish and our motives impure because of sin. Yet God desires relationship with us and seeks us out when we are in our very worst state. Amazing. Shocking. Shocking that even when we try to do the right thing, we fail. When we rely on our own understanding, we fail. Our thinking isn't right; it can't be, because we are not God. In the innocent state Adam and Eve were in prior to their fall, they had perfect communion with God. He desires us to be restored to that place of perfect and complete communion, to be one with Him. Jesus, being fully God and one with Him, as a man in the flesh, did not rely on his own thinking but said that He only did what He saw the Father doing and only spoke what He heard the Father speak, not His own words. He was in right relationship.

In Leviticus we read, "I will walk among you and be your God, and you shall be my people" (Lev. 26:12 NKJV). This statement shows us clearly that God desires we acknowledge and accept Him as God—holy, omnipotent, omnipresent, creator of all; worthy of all adoration, honor, glory, and praise. It also shows that He desires a people for Himself—those who accept Him as their god.

God created the angels for worship, and one-third fell along with Satan due to pride-wanting glory for themselves, wanting to be their own god. They fell to earth, and destruction ensued. God in His goodness desired to restore earth to its original intent. Man was created to restore the glory of God to the earth. We were in Christ before the world was formed (Eph. 1:4; 2 Ti. 1:9). God, beforehand, knew what would happen and why it would be necessary for us to participate in His story.

> Blessed be the God and Father of our Lord Jesus Christ, who hath blessed us with all spiritual blessings in heavenly places in Christ: According as he hath chosen us in him before the foundation of the world, that we should be holy and without blame before him in love: Having predestinated us unto the adoption of children by Jesus Christ to himself, according to the good pleasure of his will.
>
> Ephesians 1:3–5 (KJV)

> But we speak the wisdom of God in a mystery, even the hidden wisdom, which God ordained before the world unto our glory: Which none of the princes of this world knew: for had they known it, they would not have cruci-

fied the Lord of glory. But as it is written, Eye hath not seen, nor ear heard, neither have entered into the heart of man, the things which God hath prepared for them that love him.

1 Corinthians 2:7–9 (KJV)

Who hath saved us, and called us with an holy calling, not according to our works, but according to his own purpose and grace, which was given us in Christ Jesus before the world began.

2 Timothy 1:9 (KJV)

In hope of eternal life, which God, that cannot lie, promised before the world began;

Titus 1:2 (KJV)

# NOAH

And GOD saw that the wickedness of man was great in the earth, and that every imagination of the thoughts of his heart was only evil continually...But Noah found grace in the eyes of the LORD. These are the generations of Noah: Noah was a just man and perfect in his generations, and Noah walked with God.

Genesis 6:5; 8–9 (KJV)

In a time where man was completely given over to evil, Noah was just and walked rightly; he walked with God. He was able to hear God, and his heart was such that He obeyed God in the midst of ridicule from all around him. He obeyed God when in the natural it seemed preposterous, and the voice of the enemy was loudly stating that it was foolish to build a boat when there had never been rain. Noah believed God more than others and more than what the circumstances seemed to be. When God's judgment came upon the earth, Noah and his family were delivered. God is always looking for one whose heart is perfect toward Him, to show Himself strong on their behalf (2 Chron. 14:2, 16:9; 1 Pet. 3:12). He is the same—yesterday, today, and forever. He is even now looking for one whose heart is perfect toward Him—trusting Him, trusting that He is good. God's desire is to pour out Himself on us and for us to be one in heart and mind with Him so that this earth can be blessed as He intended, bringing glory to His name. This is right relationship—recognizing God as God, letting Him be God, and giving Him glory in our lives.

# ABRAHAM

Art not thou our God, who didst drive out the inhabitants of this land before thy people Israel, and gavest it to the seed of Abraham thy friend forever?

2 Chronicles 20:7 (KJV)

But thou, Israel, art my servant, Jacob whom I have chosen, the seed of Abraham my friend.

Isaiah 41:8 (KJV)

And the scripture was fulfilled which saith, Abraham believed God, and it was imputed unto him for righteousness: and he was called the Friend of God.

James 2:23 (KJV)

What makes Abraham God's friend? Relationship—He listened to God. In the very first instance when God spoke to Abraham and told him to go forth from all that he knew, Abraham listened and obeyed, not knowing where he was going. He was from a pagan nation of idolaters, but he instantly recognized the voice of God.

> Now the Lord had said unto Abram, Get thee out of thy
> country, and from thy kindred, and from thy father's house,
> unto a land that I will shew thee: And I will make of thee
> a great nation, and I will bless thee, and make thy name
> great; and thou shalt be a blessing: And I will bless them
> that bless thee, and curse him that curseth thee: and in
> thee shall all families of the earth be blessed. So Abram
> departed, as the Lord had spoken unto him; and Lot
> went with him: and Abram was seventy and five years old
> when he departed out of Haran.
>
> Genesis 12:1–4 (kjv)

God is always looking for one who will hear His voice and obey, that His purposes can be fulfilled on the earth.

What else makes a friend? A friend can ask us to do things, and we will do them just on the basis of friendship alone. Abraham was obedient—He did what God said.

> And the Lord said, Shall I hide from Abraham that thing
> which I do; Seeing that Abraham shall surely become a
> great and mighty nation, and all the nations of the earth
> shall be blessed in him? For I know him, that he will com-
> mand his children and his household after him, and they
> shall keep the way of the Lord, to do justice and judg-
> ment; that the Lord may bring upon Abraham that which
> he hath spoken of him.
>
> Genesis 18:17–19 (kjv)

Even when God told Abraham to offer Isaac, the child of promise, as a sacrifice, he was obedient. Abraham took his family and journeyed to the place God told him to go—Moriah, which means "chosen by Jehovah." On the third day of the journey, Abraham lifted his eyes and saw the place far off then told those that were with him to stay, that he and Isaac were going to worship. On the third day, Jesus rose from the dead. Jesus was sacrificed for us. I believe that Abraham had his spiritual eyes opened to see beyond the natural, into the realm where God's Word creates and produces, and that all that He says becomes yea and amen. Jesus is the Word made flesh, dwelling among us. Abraham believed God's promise to Him that He would make a great nation from Isaac.

> And Isaac spake unto Abraham his father, and said, My father: and he said, Here am I, my son. And he said, Behold the fire and the wood: but where is the lamb for a burnt offering? And Abraham said, My son, God will provide himself a lamb for a burnt offering: so they went both of them together.
>
> Genesis 22:7–8 (KJV)

It is not insignificant that Abraham said that God will provide himself a lamb. Jesus is the lamb of God, sacrificed for our sins. Abraham offered His son in obedience; His faith in God's Word to him was strong and sure. God responded to Abraham's faith by providing the lamb. In the society that Abraham came from, human sacrifice, especially of children, was commonplace, to gain favor with the gods by providing a human to pacify them in their anger. God is showing Abraham that human sacrifice is not His way, that the old mindsets and belief systems must be done away with. For those with eyes to see, God reveals His intense desire that we be one with Him. His desire for this is so strong that He incarnates as man on earth to become the lamb that is slain to take away the sins of the world.

What determines who our closest friends are? It is those with whom we are most like-minded…they think like us. They understand us and keep us on track with who we are. Abraham had such a close relationship with God that he reasoned with God and God changed His mind when He was set to destroy all the people in Sodom and Gomorrah. Amazing. Shocking! Abraham was such a friend of God that God would listen as Abraham reasoned with him. Abraham's interceding brought about deliverance for his nephew Lot, who was walking righteously at the time (Gen. 18:20–33).

## MOSES

"And the Lord spake unto Moses face to face, as a man speaketh unto his friend" (Ex. 33:11 KJV). We will be looking very closely at Moses's life and his relationship with God in the ensuing chapters.

## JESUS

> For God so loved the world, that he gave his only begotten Son, that whosoever believeth in him should not perish, but have everlasting life. For God sent not his Son into the world to condemn the world; but that the world through him might be saved.
>
> John 3:16–17 (KJV)

Clearly, God wants relationship with us. "But God commendeth his love toward us, in that, even while we were yet sinners, Christ died for us" (Rom. 5:8 KJV). God's desire for us has nothing to do with our goodness or our works for Him. He loved us and sent Christ to die for us while we were sinners, not after we got cleaned up. God knew beforehand that we would sin; it is in our nature from the fall of man in Adam and Eve. Yet Revelation 13:8 tells us that even before man began his sojourn on earth, God had a plan to reconcile us to Himself, through the blood of the lamb slain from the foundation of the world.

His desire and intent is to reconcile us to relationship with Him, to restore us and fulfill His purposes for our lives.

> Ye are my friends, if ye do whatsoever I command you. Henceforth I call you not servants; for the servant knoweth not what his lord doeth: but I have called you friends; for all things that I have heard of my Father I have made known unto you. Ye have not chosen me, but I have chosen

you, and ordained you, that ye should go and bring forth
fruit, and that your fruit should remain: that whatsoever
ye shall ask of the Father in my name, he may give it you.

John 15:14–16 (KJV)

Here again, we see that God is looking for a people that will
obey His voice. His voice brings life and His life in us bears much
fruit, fruit that produces seed for faith in others' lives, bearing
forth His Kingdom to this earth.

## Shocking: God Knows What Will Come Our Way throughout the Day; His Meat Will Meet Our Need

We need fresh bread daily. We don't know what the day will
bring, but God does, and He has the food that we will need to get
through it. John 4:32–34(KJV) states, "But he said unto them, I
have meat to eat that ye know not of. Therefore said the disciples
one to another, Hath any man brought him ought to eat? Jesus
saith unto them, My meat is to do the will of him that sent me,
and to finish his work."

It had been long and hot; what should have been an eleven-
day journey took forty years. The people were murmuring and
complaining. How often do we start out listening closely to God,
recognizing we can't do anything without Him, then after some
years (or months, days, sometimes even moments), it becomes
commonplace, and we think we know Him and His ways. That
is the place of danger. When we rely on our own understanding,
or on yesterday's manna. The manna was given in only one day's
allotment; it had to be gathered in the dew of the morning and
eaten before the heat of the day rotted it. Fresh revelation, He
being our first priority, is necessary to walk in the Spirit. We need
to get His truth into our spirit, chewing it so that it digests and
permeates throughout our being, before the trials of the day come
our way. If God has a word for us in the morning, and we haven't

taken the time to prepare ourselves to receive it, we may not be able to eat it later after the heat of the day has gotten to us and our emotions are frazzled, our stomach is in a knot, and our mind is overheated.

You never know when God may bring someone along your path who may need the Word you received that morning. It may not have been for you at all, but to be fed to another. In my devotion time one morning, the Lord led me to a passage of scripture that did not seem to apply to my life in any way. In fact, I felt rather dry and empty as I went to work. As the day progressed, a coworker came into my office and began sharing things that were in her heart. The scripture passage I had received that morning directly related to her situation. I shared with her what God had shown me, and she was astounded, encouraged, and motivated to share it with others.

I was blown away by God's working through me in this way. My sharing the Word with her brought life into my dry bones also, not directly from the Word, but from the reality of His overwhelming goodness and omniscience—He knew what she would need and orchestrated her day and mine so that her need would be met and I would receive greater revelation of His intimate knowledge of us and His desire to relate to us and fulfill His purpose in and through us. In this instance, I received my meat from sharing the Word.

His meat for you may be to minister to someone, to hear the voice of God by the Holy Spirit and speak to them a word of knowledge. That is what Jesus did with the woman at the well (John 4). Jesus revealed Himself to the woman at the well as Christ, able to perceive by the Spirit all she had done in her life to try and fill the deepest need. His disciples came to him after going into town to buy food. Seeing Him at the well with the woman, they entreated him to go eat, and He said, "I have food to eat that you know not of, my meat is to do the will of Him who sent me and to finish His work." Clearly, He is communicating that when you are doing the Father's will, the work of the Kingdom, He himself will be your food. Jesus said He is the bread of heaven in John 6:32–33. Our food may be the Word, ministry, or worship of the king. These are the foods that feed our spirit! Put God first and let Him orchestrate your day; be sensitive to His leading, overcome your fleshly desires and perhaps you will be fed with the hidden manna referred to in Revelation 2:17.

## Shocking: God Used a Prostitute to Save His People—Faith Is the Only Requirement

### RAHAB

It is solely about faith, not who we are or what we do in our own strength. Our salvation depends on believing on the one true god and doing His will. In Joshua, chapter 2, we find an incredible account of a prostitute used by God to deliver his people from the hands of the enemy:

> And Joshua the son of Nun sent out of Shittim two men to spy secretly, saying, Go look over the land, even Jericho. And they went and came to the house of a harlot named Rahab. And they stayed there. And the king of Jericho was told about it, saying, Behold, men from the sons of Israel came in here tonight, to search out the country. And the king of Jericho sent to Rahab, saying, Bring out the men that have come to you, those who have entered into your house. For they have come to search out all the country. And the woman took the two men and hid them. And she said, Two men came to me, but I did not know from where they came. And it happened when it was dark, at the time of shutting the gate, the men went out. Where the men went I do not know. Go after them quickly, for you shall overtake them. But she had brought them up on the roof, and had hidden them with the stalks of flax which she had laid in order upon the roof. And the men

went after them on the way to Jordan, to the fords. And when they who pursued them had gone out, they shut the gate. And before they had laid down, she came up to them on the roof. And she said to the men, I know that Jehovah has given you the land, and that your terror has fallen on us, and that all those who live in the land faint because of you. For we have heard how Jehovah dried up the water of the Red Sea for you when you came out of Egypt, and what you did to the two kings of the Amorites that were on the other side Jordan, Sihon and Og, whom you utterly destroyed. And we had heard, and our hearts melted, nor did any more spirit remain in any man, because of you. For Jehovah your God, He is God in Heaven above and in earth beneath. Now therefore, I pray you, swear to me by Jehovah, since I have dealt with you in kindness, that you will also deal with kindness to my father's house. And give me a true token, and shall save alive my father and my mother, and my brothers and my sisters, and all that they have, and deliver our lives from death. And the men answered her, Our life shall be for yours, if you do not tell our business. And when Jehovah has given us the land, we will deal kindly and truly with you. Then she let them go down by a cord through the window. For her house was on the town wall, and she lived on the wall. And she said to them, Get up into the mountain lest the pursuers meet you. And hide yourselves there three days until the pursuers have returned. And afterward you may go your way. And the men said to her, We will be blameless of this oath to you which you have made us swear. Behold, when we come into the land, you shall set this line of scarlet thread in the window from which you let us down. And you shall bring your father and your mother, and your brothers, and all your father's household, home to you. And it shall be, whoever shall go out of the doors of your house, his blood shall be on his head, and we will be blameless. And whoever shall be with you in the house, his blood shall be on our head if a hand is on him. And if you tell our business, then we will be free of the oath which you have made us swear to you. And she said, Let it be according to your word. And she sent them away, and they departed. And she set the scarlet line in the window. And they went and came to the mountain, and stayed there three days until the pursuers had returned. And the pursuers looked for them throughout all the way, but did not find them. And the two men returned and came down from the mountain, and passed over, and came to Joshua the son of Nun. And they told him all that happened to them. And they said to Joshua, Truly Jehovah has delivered all the land into our hands, for even all those who live in the country faint because of us.

Joshua 2:1–24 (MJKV)

Rahab had heard of the accounts of God's faithfulness to the Israelites and believed that the God of the Israelites was the Lord God. She aided His servants, asking that they repay her with their kindness and that her whole family be saved when Jericho was destroyed. Amazingly, shockingly, Rahab was in the lineage of Jesus Christ (Matthew, chapter 1) and is hallmarked in Hebrews 11:31 and James 2:25 as an example of walking in faith. Think about this. God intended to use a prostitute. He shocks us into the reality of the greatness of His love. Romans 9 declares that the Gentiles received salvation when Israel didn't—why? Faith, not works of righteousness, is the requirement. The Gentiles received righteousness through faith; this is the only way, and it is available to all who believe on the finished work of Christ on the cross. Paul states it well in his first letter to the Corinthians:

But God hath chosen the foolish things of the world to confound the wise; and God hath chosen the weak things of the world to confound the things which are mighty; And base things of the world, and things which are despised, hath God chosen, yea, and things which are not, to bring to nought things that are: That no flesh should glory in his presence. But of him are ye in Christ Jesus, who of God is made unto us wisdom, and righteousness, and sanctification, and redemption: That, according as it is written, He that glorieth, let him glory in the Lord

1 Corinthians 1:27–31 (KJV)

Shocking: God intends to use the base, despised, foolish, and weak of this world to bring about His purposes. We will probably be very surprised when we get to heaven; many of those who seemed good in our eyes will be absent, and we will see many that we never would have thought would make it there.

There are many prophetic insights in the account of Rahab.

- Rahab hid the men in the flax. Flax is symbolic of the weakness of man. Our weaknesses are hidden when we walk in faith.

- Rahab had strong discernment. Joshua had been told (Joshua 1:10–11) that in three days they would pass over. Rahab heard the same thing; in Joshua 2: 16, she told them to hide three days in the mountain then pass over. Prophetically, three days signifies the resurrection power of God. The third day is when they were empowered to cross over.

- Joshua's men told Rahab to hang a scarlet thread from her window so that she would be spared. The scarlet thread representing shed blood hung from the window, as with the Passover when shed blood was marked over the doorposts. She and her household were spared from death.

Rahab is also an account where we learn that when we are protecting the people of God against their enemies, it is okay to lie. Shocking. God allows breaking of the commandment when it is to further His purposes, when it is to foil the plans of His enemies. There are other instances. In Exodus 1:15–21, the midwives lied to Pharaoh in order to save the Hebrew babies. In 2 Kings 6:19, Elisha lied to divert God's enemies onto another path.

I think the most interesting and thought-provoking example is when Paul refers to his lie, "For if the truth of God hath more abounded through my lie unto his glory; why yet am I also judged as a sinner?" (Rom. 3:7 KJV)

He doesn't tell us what the lie is, but he has been preaching that circumcision is of the heart in Romans 2:24–29. In Acts 15:1–6, we read that Paul preached strongly against the necessity of circumcision among the Gentiles, yet after that (Acts 16:3), he himself circumcised Timothy so as not to offend the Jews. Perhaps this is the lie? We don't know for sure, but it is certainly plain by his language in Romans 3:7 that he feels it is okay to lie when furthering the gospel.

Genesis 12:3 tells us that He will bless those who bless His people. Is this a principle that includes lying if necessary in order to bless them, as in Rahab's case? Just a question to consider: I am not in any way promoting lying, I am simply pointing out that God's thoughts are higher than ours and that, perhaps, furthering His purposes is highest.

> Now the LORD had said unto Abram, Get thee out of thy country, and from thy kindred, and from thy father's house, unto a land that I will shew thee: And I will make of thee a great nation, and I will bless thee, and make thy name great; and thou shalt be a blessing: And I will bless them that bless thee, and curse him that curseth thee: and in thee shall all families of the earth be blessed.
>
> Genesis 12:1–3 (KJV)

In Psalm 115 we read of an incredibly beautiful promise for those that fear the Lord:

> O Israel, trust thou in the LORD: he is their help and their shield. O house of Aaron, trust in the LORD: he is their help and their shield. Ye that fear the LORD, trust in the LORD: he is their help and their shield. The LORD hath been mindful of us: he will bless us; he will bless the house

of Israel; he will bless the house of Aaron. He will bless them that fear the LORD, both small and great. The LORD shall increase you more and more, you and your children. Ye are blessed of the LORD which made heaven and earth.

Psalms 115:9–15 (KJV)

What is faith but believing in and trusting in the Lord? This is what He requires of us. We are all in a place of transition as we move from glory to glory. We are all sinners, and every sin, no matter how small or large, stems from our heart and keeps us separated from Him. Without faith it is impossible to please Him. So all the "right" actions don't please Him, only our faith. We would do well to remember that He is the author and finisher of our faith, and that He alone is perfect and worthy to be the judge of our eternal destiny.

## Shocking: If It Looks Like a Duck and Sounds Like a Duck, It Doesn't Mean It Is a Duck

### JEROBOAM'S SIN

But Omri wrought evil in the eyes of the LORD, and did worse than all that were before him. For he walked in all the way of Jeroboam the son of Nebat, and in his sin wherewith he made Israel to sin, to provoke the LORD God of Israel to anger with their vanities.

1 Kings 16:25–26 (KJV)

Omri in the Hebrew language means heaping, sheaves, to gather grain to make merchandise of it.[1] Omri gathered the people to himself to make merchandise of them for his profit.

What are vanities? The word vanities in Strong's Concordance means emptiness, something transitory, and unsatisfactory; vain; the root means to be vain in act, word or expectation; to lead astray.[2]

According to Webster's Dictionary, the meaning of vanity can include the quality or condition of being vain, preoccupation with or excessive pride in one's appearance or accomplishments, conceit; lack of usefulness, worth or effect; hollowness; futility; worthlessness.[3]

Some of the definitions for vain include having no real value, ineffectiveness, not yielding the desired outcome, unsuccessful, futile, fruitless, lacking substance or worth, hollow, idle; showing undue preoccupation with or pride in one's appearance or accomplishments.[4]

So we see that we provoke God when we are occupied with vain purposes, fruitless activities, and worthless endeavors. If you are a teacher or leader, the greater responsibility is on you as you cause many others to sin by your influence. The only fruit that remains and is worthwhile is in Christ; not in vain, religious acts that make us feel pious or better than others.

Omri walked in the ways of Jeroboam. What did Jeroboam do that was so bad? In 1 Kings 12, we read that Jereboam turned Israel away from God by creating false gods so they wouldn't go the distance and spend the time necessary to worship the one true God. He created idols that were easier to worship. He also set up his own feasts similar to God's ordained feasts and set priests from the lowest of the people, not of the house of Levi, which was what God mandated.

Jeroboam's sin was in making the lowest people priests, even himself, and making idols so as to have the kingdom for himself. He didn't want the people going to Jerusalem to worship, so he made golden calves and used human reasoning—how much easier it is to worship here, not to make any effort.

Levi in the Hebrew language means attached, united, twined.[5] Levites are attached to God and His purposes, dedicating their lives to Him as His priests on the earth..

Jehu gives another example of creating idols for false worship.

Howbeit from the sins of Jeroboam the son of Nebat, who made Israel to sin, Jehu departed not from after them, to wit, the golden calves that were in Bethel, and that were in Dan. And the LORD said unto Jehu, Because thou hast done well in executing that which is right in mine eyes, and hast done unto the house of Ahab according to all that was in mine heart, thy children of the fourth generation shall sit on the throne of Israel. But Jehu took no heed to walk in the law of the LORD God of Israel with all his heart: for he departed not from the sins of Jeroboam, which made Israel to sin.

2 Kings 10:29–31 (KJV)

The word calves in Strong's Concordance notes that the word calf is used as "frisking around," and the root comes from a word meaning to revolve or be circular.[6]

The enemy's strategy is to seduce through pride and seek after empty things that bear no eternal fruit, causing us to become attached to vain endeavors and go around in circles (as the children of Israel spent forty years wandering for an eleven-day journey). The distractions will be easier to do, based on our own accomplishments, but be futile and worthless. They will "seem reasonable" to our natural minds. Good is often the enemy of the best. "Frisking around" also implies playfulness, not taking things seriously; in modern day terms, "playing church" rather than recognizing the holiness of God and being in right relationship with Him.

The application for leaders is the danger of using God's favor and gifts to bring honor to self, any form of manipulation rather than following God fully, His way. Jehu destroyed Baal and all the Baal worshippers, which was good. Baal was the god of fertility and nature. Yet he continued Jereboam's practice of worshipping false gods—the golden calves. The Israelites believed in the one true god, but they were taken in by a false image of Him—a replica, an image to worship rather than relationship, a form of godliness, denying the power thereof. This is religion at its worst, continuing with form and ritual and not even recognizing that God isn't in it.

Churches today do this when trying to gain followers and keep people from going elsewhere, by trying to please man rather than God, using God's gifts for their own benefit – saying what they think will please people and keep them happy, and their money coming in. There is a danger of creating a false image, a replica, a form that is one-dimensional and static, comfortable, safe and familiar or by appointing people to positions that God has not qualified them to so that they will stay in the church (Gal. 1:10; 1 Thess. 2:4-6).

In 2 Kings 13, 1-10, we read that a man of God out of Judah came to Jeroboam by the word of the Lord and prophesied that Josiah, of the house of David, would destroy the false altars and false priests, and that as a sign, the altar would be rent and the ashes poured out. As soon as he said this, Jeroboam sought to lay hold of him and his right hand withered, the altar was rent and ashes poured out. The right hand represents authority; God was showing He has greater authority than Jeroboam, and this was confirmed by the word of the man of God manifesting immediately. What was Jeroboam's response? He asked the man of God to pray unto his god that his hand be restored, which it was. Jeroboam was so grateful that he desired to give a reward and asked the man of God to come home with him for refreshments.

What follows is an even more chilling account of the danger of not listening to the voice of God and being deceived by those that look and sound like the "real thing." It is so shocking that I am listing the full account in its entirety.

> And the king said unto the man of God, Come home with me, and refresh thyself, and I will give thee a reward. And the man of God said unto the king, If thou wilt give me half thine house, I will not go in with thee, neither will I eat bread nor drink water in this place: For so was

it charged me by the word of the Lᴏʀᴅ, saying, Eat no bread, nor drink water, nor turn again by the same way that thou camest. So he went another way, and returned not by the way that he came to Bethel. Now there dwelt an old prophet in Bethel; and his sons came and told him all the works that the man of God had done that day in Bethel: the words which he had spoken unto the king, them they told also to their father. And their father said unto them, What way went he? For his sons had seen what way the man of God went, which came from Judah. And he said unto his sons, Saddle me the ass. So they saddled him the ass: and he rode thereon, And went after the man of God, and found him sitting under an oak: and he said unto him, Art thou the man of God that camest from Judah? And he said, I am. Then he said unto him, Come home with me, and eat bread. And he said, I may not return with thee, nor go in with thee: neither will I eat bread nor drink water with thee in this place: For it was said to me by the word of the Lᴏʀᴅ, Thou shalt eat no bread nor drink water there, nor turn again to go by the way that thou camest. He said unto him, I am a prophet also as thou art; and an angel spake unto me by the word of the Lᴏʀᴅ, saying, Bring him back with thee into thine house, that he may eat bread and drink water. But he lied unto him. So he went back with him, and did eat bread in his house, and drank water. And it came to pass, as they sat at the table, that the word of the Lᴏʀᴅ came unto the prophet that brought him back: And he cried unto the man of God that came from Judah, saying, Thus saith the Lᴏʀᴅ, Forasmuch as thou hast disobeyed the mouth of the Lᴏʀᴅ, and hast not kept the commandment which the Lᴏʀᴅ thy God commanded thee, But camest back, and hast eaten bread and drunk water in the place, of the which the Lᴏʀᴅ did say to thee, Eat no bread, and drink no water; thy carcase shall not come unto the sepulchre of thy fathers. And it came to pass, after he had eaten bread, and after he had drunk, that he saddled for him the ass, to wit, for the prophet whom he had brought back. And when he was gone, a lion met him by the way, and slew him: and his carcase was cast in the way, and the ass stood by it, the lion also stood by the carcase. And, behold, men passed by, and saw the carcase cast in the way, and the lion standing by the carcase: and they came and told it in the city where the old prophet dwelt. And when the prophet that brought him back from the way heard thereof, he said, It is the man of God, who was disobedient unto the word of the Lord: therefore the Lord hath delivered him unto the lion, which hath torn him, and slain him, according to the word of the Lord, which he spake unto him. And he spake to his sons, Saddle me the ass. And they saddled him. And he went and found his carcase cast in the way, and the ass and the lion standing by the carcase: the lion had not eaten the carcase, nor torn the ass. And the prophet took up the carcase of the man of God, and laid it upon the ass, and brought it back: and the old prophet came to the city, to mourn and to bury him. And he laid his carcase in his own grave; and they mourned over him, saying, Alas, my brother! And it came to pass, after he had buried him, that he spake to his sons, saying, When I am dead, then bury me in the sepulchre wherein the man of God is buried; lay my bones beside his bones: For the saying which he cried by the word of the Lord against the altar in Bethel, and against all the houses of the high places which are in the cities of Samaria, shall surely come to pass. After this thing Jeroboam returned not from his evil way, but made again of the lowest of the people priests of the high places: whosoever would, he consecrated him, and he became one of the priests of the high places. And this thing became sin unto the house of Jeroboam, even to cut it off, and to destroy it from off the face of the earth.

1Kings 13:7-34 (KJV)

Wow. Here we have a man of God standing on the word of the Lord in the face of the King, when it was offered him an opportunity for reward, then immediately being deceived by one who looks and sounds like the real thing. In fact, this "old prophet" was a prophet. Perhaps the man of God from Judah even knew him or knew of him. Certainly he spoke with the voice of authority, saying that an angel of the Lord spoke to him by the word of the Lord. This swayed the man of God from Judah to discount what he had heard from the Lord, a clear example of someone that looks right and sounds right but isn't right.

There are a lot of questions that could be asked – why did the old prophet lie? Was it a test for the man of God? He had stood strong on the word before the King, but failed to stand strong before another prophet. How much easier it would be to rely on others to hear from God, but we have to be able to hear from Him ourselves so that we know when others speak whether it is confirmation or false. In Galatians 1:8-9, Paul warns us, "But though we, or an angel from heaven, preach any other gospel unto you than that which we have preached unto you, let him be accursed. As we said before, so say I now again, If any man preach any other gospel unto you than that ye have received, let him be accursed." Also in 2 Corinthians 11:13-15, we are warned, "For such are false apostles, deceitful workers, transforming themselves into the apostles of Christ. And no marvel; for Satan himself is transformed into an angel of light. Therefore it is no great thing if his ministers also be transformed as the ministers of righteousness; whose end shall be according to their works."

Another shocking point in this is that the prophet himself rebuked the man of God for listening to his own lie! Also shocking is the punishment – to be killed by a lion. This was a man of God from Judah. A lion is a symbol of Judah! It is as if the holiness of God within him, the roaring of the lion prevailed as judgment against the act of disobedience. I think this is confirmed as supernatural symbolism by the fact that the lion stood guard over the body, the lion did not eat the carcass and did not attack those passing by or the ass that also stood by. The lion himself was on assignment, sent by God to invoke this judgment, and did not go beyond his orders. Amazing.

Additionally shocking is that the old prophet, when he heard of the death, came and took the carcass and placed it in his own sepulcher and told his servants that when he died, he was to be placed with him. He recognized that the man of God from Judah was a true prophet, and that even though he was slain, his words would be fulfilled. Amazing account, and sobering. It is a fearful thing to fall into the hands of the living God (Heb. 10:31).

We must be discerning and hear from God so that we won't be led astray by well-meaning people who think they are hearing from God, or deceived by false prophets, wolves, or those with the spirit of antichrist or religion (Matt. 7:15, 24:11; Luke 6:26; 2 Pet. 2:1; 1 John 4:1). If leaders, it is so important to stay humbly before the face of God to ensure that we aren't being influenced by the wrong spirit and/or wrong motives and become those very things ourselves.

# SHOCKING: THE REALITY THAT HIS WAYS ARE NOT OUR WAYS

## Shocking: God's Ways Are Vision, Virtue, and Verity

First, He gives us a vision of what He wants to do. Second, He then works it out in our character (virtue) so that we can hold more of His presence and bring His kingdom purposes to pass. Third, the vision becomes reality.

> And Moses was learned in all the wisdom of the Egyptians, and was mighty in words and in deeds. And when he was full forty years old, it came into his heart to visit his brethren the children of Israel. And seeing one of them suffer wrong, he defended him, and avenged him that was oppressed, and smote the Egyptian: For he supposed his brethren would have understood how that God by his hand would deliver them: but they understood not. And the next day he shewed himself unto them as they strove, and would have set them at one again, saying, Sirs, ye are brethren; why do ye wrong one to another? But he that did his neighbor wrong thrust him away, saying, "Who made thee a ruler and a judge over us? Wilt thou kill me, as thou diddest the Egyptian yesterday?"
>
> Acts 7:22–28 (KJV)

Moses at forty years of age struck the Egyptian and killed him; he was then forty years in the desert with God; it also took forty years for the Israelites to enter the Promised Land. Moses tried to deliver his oppressed brethren in his own strength and understanding. Afterward, he had to spend forty years in a wilderness experience, learning to wait and hear God's voice. This is like our Christian experience. God shows us our gifts and gives a vision of where He is taking us, and we run forward in our own strength trying to make it happen, making a mess because it isn't God's timing, or creating a monster that we have to uphold in our own strength, which ultimately fails. Then we have to learn to wait and listen to God's voice, in every moment.

The beautiful, glorious truth of the goodness of God is that those areas in our lives where it seems the greatest sin occurred, God will turn into an asset for His purposes, once we let Him lead us. Our weaknesses become strength in God's hands, as we learn to trust Him. Moses's pride at the knowledge that he was to be a deliverer led him to the rash act of murdering the Egyptian. However, in turn, this caused him to run into the wilderness where he learned meekness. His dual nature (a Hebrew raised as an Egyptian) created self-doubt as to his identity, skepticism that his words would be believed. In our Christian walk, how often our dual nature (flesh and spirit) causes us to doubt that anyone would listen to us. Our pride causes our sin, and God in his mercy and love teaches us so that we are humbled and put back into the right relationship with Him as God and us as His people. Recognize the beauty in our sin—it causes us to turn to the Lord.

Recognition of our weaknesses, the sin to which we are prone keeps us humble and dependent on Him. Not doing so will bring an opportunity for Satan to bring a temptation that will be disguised so that we will not recognize it. Remember that one of his tactics in these last days is to wear out the saints (Dan. 7:25). The term "wear out" comes from the root word meaning to afflict, to mentally fail, decay, consume, spent, waste. The enemy wants to have us become consumed with other things that will distract us from our purpose and decay our spirit life until there is nothing left. It is a subtle, slow process, so slow we don't recognize it until it we are nearly succumbed. We can become so busy with interests, even "God" interests, that we do not give ourselves the quiet time to hear His still, small voice. Often when we are worn out our mind is so overwhelmed that we cannot hear a thing but our own flesh screaming because we haven't taken care of ourselves.

This happened to me, and I thank God that He delivered me out of it just in time. The Holy Spirit had been speaking in His still, small voice, but I had been feeding my flesh and soul—my natural man—more than my spirit. I was in a position of increasing responsibility in my career, a position He had brought me into and in it had brought favor and promotion to me. Yet it had become mine along the way, giving me a name and purpose. It became my identity, rather than Christ.

In addition, my husband Kerry and I had not been spending time on our marriage. We weren't paying attention, just cruising on autopilot. We knew that God brought us together for a purpose but weren't taking care and devoting time to it. Early in our relationship, we had an incredible visitation from the Lord. Together—the manifest presence of God was so strong between us as we read the Word that the air was thick and shimmering with his glory. We had a vision of our marriage and ministry. Fast-forward fifteen years. We had been used in ministry, and then it didn't look like we thought it should, and we pulled back. We were disconnected and disenchanted. This set the stage for one of the greatest trials of my life.

At work, I was overwhelmed with new responsibilities in addition to trying to maintain the previous ones. I had been leading a workgroup Bible study for eight years and recently stopped doing that, because I often worked through lunch or had meetings that ran into the lunch hour. I was so frazzled and tired I wasn't even able to hear God, as my mind was consumed with work and worry. I was not paying attention to my spiritual, physical, or emotional needs. Your emotional needs will find a way to be met. If not through people (healthy or unhealthy), it may be through overindulgences that dull the pain and emptiness momentarily, or through "busy-ness" to avoid the feelings altogether. Or the emotions may turn inward and sickness or disease may form. Many studies have been done that show a correlation between emotions and physical conditions.

I had become attached to people who were feeding my emotions, and coming into agreement about my difficult situation, rather than seeking God's provision. Huge red flag! I was on a road leading to destruction, a road that was cleverly disguised and intended to destroy me. Perhaps many arrows could have been deflected by the armor of God, but I was outside the camp of God's people and was not in fellowship or seeking godly counsel.

Praise be to God as He intervened in a drastic way. I became sick to the point of needing emergency hospitalization. In retrospect, it seemed that my body itself was exploding because of the conflict between my soul and my spirit. I found out later had I not gone to the hospital when I did I could have died. God told me by the Holy Spirit that He had picked me up and pulled me out of my workplace. He said that I was done there. So I gave my notice of retirement.

In retrospect, for over a year I had been feeling nudging to look into retirement from that position, nudging that I ignored. God was really dealing with me. It was time to make a huge change. Career had become way too important—taking priority over ministry, family, and health. I was very surprised that this had happened to me. I had never been interested in a career; when we first married I just wanted a part-time job so I could spend time with the Lord and with my family. Somewhere along the way I had gotten sidetracked. Kerry knows that he played a big part in this also. He had, at times, pushed me to advance when there was opportunity, for the money. I knew that it was over; God had told me this. It was time to be more focused on what was really important—my relationship with Him, my marriage, my children and grandchildren, and to finish the book He had told me to write! In order for me to retire, we had to make huge adjustments in our lifestyle. We put our two-story house on the market and found a smaller home close to the children and grandchildren. Amazingly, the third day our house was on the market, we got an offer above what we had at the top of our range! God clearly was smiling on this decision.

The actual retirement process took months because I wasn't just quitting, I was retiring from a government career. During this time, I struggled with the decision. I liked the accoutrements of worldly success—the money, the name, the interactions with business associates, travelling to conferences and staying in nice hotels, even the career clothes. These things, and some of the relationships, were very difficult to give up, and I tried to rationalize why it wasn't wrong. True, none of these things are wrong in themselves. For example, it isn't money that's the root all evil; it's the love of money. Having friendships with others isn't wrong, but if you are seeking to fill a need with these that only God should be filling, it will never work. The truth was that I had developed soul ties that were affecting my relationship with Kerry and my walk with God. I could not be in relationships with others in order to meet emotional needs that only God and/or my husband should be meeting!

The Holy Spirit reminded me of times in the past where I was at a similar crossroad. God was allowing this so that I could go deeper into an old wound and be healed. He was showing me lies I had come into agreement with and the walls I'd erected to keep me safe from the possibility of pain. These walls kept me from seeing the real core issues of inferiority, insecurity, and feelings of unworthiness and shame. I'd become expert at avoiding these feelings through denial, dismissal, and deflection, choosing behaviors that worked in the past but that God would not allow going forward. He was calling me to a deeper place of intimacy with Himself and my husband, breaking generational strongholds in order to release new life for us and all those in our lineage and sphere of influence.

I thank God for His grace. The Holy Spirit recently reminded me that many years ago I had an experience where God through the Holy Spirit told me that if I didn't start living for Him, I was done here on the earth (this was confirmed by my daughter through a dream she had). Remembering His warning in light of this experience is sobering. I am a firm believer that God does not "send" sickness, but if we aren't walking in His will, sickness may be a tool that is used to bring us back to Him! He creates the weapons of destruction (Jer. 6:19; Isa. 54:16), although it is our own actions, beliefs, and words that provide the enemy access. Not only did the Lord give me clear warning, I had been repeating over and over, every day for months, "The stress is killing me."

We overcome by the blood of the Lamb and the Word of our Testimony (Rev. 12:11). Remember your testimonies! It may seem that your life (carnal, soulish, flesh) is dying, and yes, it must, for the Spirit life to live through you. Do not believe the lies of the enemy, the same lie that deceived Eve in the beginning— "Did God Say?" Yes, He did. No, He is not a liar. He knows that the thief comes to kill, steal, and destroy (John 10:10), but Jesus came to give us life, and that even more abundantly. The enemy brings a false vision of the abundant life, of unity and oneness. There is only one way, and that is through the cross. The vision that God will fulfill is greater, brighter, and more fulfilling than the illusion that the enemy falsely brings. Remember your past, where the enemy took you down a road promising fulfillment that ended in bondage and addiction. Just like the first high can never be recreated, every illusion he brings is that way.

Conversely, you can rise higher and higher in the Spirit with Christ and never be disappointed. He will always fulfill, and there is always greater fulfillment as you grow in Him. He is the one you are desiring to be one with. He is the Desire of the Ages, the Rose of Sharon, the Bright and Morning Star, the Alpha and Omega. When the earth ceases to be, He is still the great "I AM

THAT I AM" (Ex. 3:14 KJV), and we are one with God through Christ, forever through eternity to reign with Him.

The illusion of the enemy, and the greatest things this earthly life can offer, are nothing in comparison to His presence, His purpose, and His Kingdom. Remember, Satan tried to tempt Christ in the same way, offering Him the kingdoms of this world, trying to tempt Him through His basic needs (make this stone into bread), through twisting God's Word to act presumptuously (jump off the cliff; the angels will save you). Jesus knew that nothing compares to eternity and that the only true life comes by obedience to God's Word. The enemy came in right after Jesus received the Word that He was God's son, and that is how the enemy tempted Him when he tried to get Jesus to move outside of God's will: "If you are the Son of God…" (Luke 4:3 KJV). Would we not be tempted to use our power as the Son of God to turn stones into bread, after forty days of fasting, being surrounded by beasts and tormented by the enemy?

Remember that when you receive a word of promise, you will be tempted. Jesus said that Satan came immediately on account of the Word, in Matthew 4:15. You must be tempted to overcome and be filled with the power of the Spirit (Luke 4:14). Jesus was sent by the Holy Spirit, full of the Spirit, into the wilderness (Luke 4:1), then tempted. Overcoming by the Word of God, he then returned in the power of the Spirit. This is our example in every test. How vital it is to know and rely on the Word of God to recognize that there will be a testing of the Word. The enemy wants to steal it from our hearts; God wants to have it take root and bear fruit in our lives for His purposes and glory.

In my case, God used that trial to show my husband and me the necessity of maintaining our relationship in all its facets and nuances. This is our first ministry. We recognize the need to have rest and maintain peace in our lives, not become overextended, and to take time to have fun doing things together. Over the course of the subsequent two years, God restored our marriage beyond what it was before. We fell in love again and became more in love than we ever were. We began to truly comprehend how God honors and blesses covenant. Now into our third year beyond the trial, God has restored, repositioned, and reconnected us to ministry where we are fitted together into the Body of Christ in a way that we could not have been before. He had many things to work out of us and other things to work into us, and we had to be properly aligned together in our marriage. He also had to deal with the hidden desire in both of us for money and fame. Had this not been worked out in the natural, it would have destroyed us and brought others down also should we become successful in ministry.

God's ways include allowing Satan to tempt us. It is part of our test. Satan wants us to fail the test. God tests where we are in relation to the vision; the trials result in godly character built into us (virtue) so that we can walk in His authority and bring His kingdom here on earth, as it is in heaven (verity).

## Shocking: You Can't Enter into the Promised Land Unless You Help Your Brother Enter

Then Joshua commanded the officers of the people saying, Pass through the host, and command the people, saying, Prepare food for yourselves, for within three days you are crossing over this Jordan, to go in to possess the land which Jehovah your God is giving you to possess it (The land is given you so that you will possess it; to occupy by driving out the previous tenants and possessing in their place; to seize, take, expel. He wants to establish His Kingdom, to take dominion in every area where He sends us.) And Joshua spoke to the Reubenites and to the Gadites and to the half tribe of Manasseh, saying: Remember the word which Moses the servant of Jehovah commanded you saying, Jehovah your God has given you rest and has given you this land. Your wives, your little ones, and your cattle shall remain in the land which Moses gave you on this side

Jordan. But you shall go armed before your brothers, all the mighty men of valor, and help them until Jehovah has given your brothers rest, even as you, and they also have possessed the land which Jehovah your God gives them; and you shall return to the land of your possession and enjoy it, which Moses Jehovah's servant gave you on this side Jordan, towards the sunrise.

Joshua 1:10–15 (NKJV)

Joshua is referencing Moses's instruction and exhortation found in Numbers 32, where Moses warned them that to stay and relax before the Jordan in their inheritance and not go over with the others to war with them, would be like those at Kadesh Barnea who gave an evil report and discouraged the others. It would be tempting to stay and relax because it was a good land for their cattle right where they were—they were comfortable and prosperous. It would have been discouraging to the others for them to stay there, and it also would be a sin against the land, and their sin would find them out. Even the land has a voice—in Romans 8:22, we read that all creation is groaning, waiting for the manifestation of the sons of God. Jesus said the rocks would cry out if the people didn't praise Him (Luke 19:40). The blood cried out from the land when Cain killed Abel (Gen. 4:10).

When God is calling the church forward to take possession, there is an expectation for the whole body to receive. If one has conquered, is blessed, and in a resting place, he will be expected to use his weapons forged in war to help others enter also. The parable of the talents would apply (Matt. 25:14–29). Also Jesus's life—he didn't esteem himself worthy of the inheritance, but humbled himself to become a servant of all (Phil. 2:5–8; Heb. 2:9–10).

Take heed, brothers, lest there be in any of you an evil heart of unbelief, in departing from the living God. But exhort one another daily, while it is called today, lest any of you be hardened through the deceitfulness of sin. For we

are made partakers of Christ, if we hold the beginning of
our confidence steadfast to the end.

Heb. 3:12–14 (nkjv)

For every high priest taken from among men is ordained
for men in the things pertaining to God, so that he may
offer both gifts and sacrifices for sins, who can have compassion on the ignorant and on those who are out of the
way. For he himself also is compassed with weakness.

Hebrews 5:1–2 (nkjv)

The priest intercedes for those who can't enter the Holiest of
Holies yet. We are all kings and priests. To walk in the priestly
anointing we must intercede for others.

Moreover as for me, God forbid that I should sin against
the Lord in ceasing to pray for you: but I will teach you
the good and the right way:

1 Samuel 12:23 (kjv)

And the Lord turned the captivity of Job, when he prayed
for his friends: also the Lord gave Job twice as much as
he had before.

Job 42:10 (kjv)

But I say unto you, Love your enemies, bless them that
curse you, do good to them that hate you, and pray for
them which despitefully use you, and persecute you;

Matthew 5:44 (kjv)

Remember those who are in bonds, as bound with them, those
who suffer adversity, as being yourselves also in the body.

Hebrews 13:3 (nkjv)

> Confess your faults one to another, and pray one for another, that ye may be healed. The effectual fervent prayer of a righteous man availeth much.
>
> James 5:16 (KJV)

Along with praying for others, we need to exhort one another daily (Heb. 3:13). We should share our testimonies with others and encourage them to keep moving forward. It is critical to our walk that we have godly men and women who will remind us of where we've come from, not just in our personal lives, but back to the roots of faith. That is why Hebrews 11 exhorts us to remember the historical faith walk of those gone before us. In the Israelites' journey, we see that when a godly leader died, the people turned back. There will always be leaders and followers. For those who God has called to be leaders, how imperative that we walk circumspectly, recognizing that there are sheep scattered and following anything that remotely suggests help. Yet even if you aren't a leader, you are a sister or a brother, and yes, you are your brother's keeper!

## Shocking: Circumcision Is a Shocking Allegory; As We Allow Our Flesh to Be Cut Away, the Reproach Is Rolled Away from Our Lives

The Israelites failed to circumcise their children in the wilderness. They were hardened spiritually; they had allowed the mixed multitude in their midst to influence them and were not mindful of the things of God. If you do not stand firm on the truth, the lies others believe and speak will influence your heart. What you hear enters into your heart through your ears. Speak truth and combat the lies that you have heard! Your heart needs to be reinforced with truth. Peter denied Jesus three times. Later, Jesus had Peter respond to the question "Do you love me?" three times. This countered the lies that Peter had spoken and placed Peter's heart back into alignment with truth.

> At that time the LORD said unto Joshua, Make thee sharp knives, and circumcise again the children of Israel the second time. And Joshua made him sharp knives, and circumcised the children of Israel at the hill of the foreskins. And this is the cause why Joshua did circumcise: All the people that came out of Egypt, that were males, even all the men of war, died in the wilderness by the way, after they came out of Egypt. Now all the people that came out were circumcised: but all the people that were born in the wilderness by the way as they came forth out of Egypt, them they had not circumcised. For the children of Israel walked forty years in the wilderness, till all the people that were men of war, which came out of Egypt, were consumed, because they obeyed not the voice of the LORD: unto whom the LORD sware that he would not shew them the land, which the LORD sware unto their fathers that he would give us, a land that floweth with milk and honey. And their children, whom he raised up in their stead, them Joshua circumcised: for they were uncircumcised, because they had not circumcised them by the way. And it came to pass, when they had done circumcising all the people, that they abode in their places in the camp, till they were whole. And the LORD said unto Joshua, This day have I rolled away the reproach of Egypt from off you. Wherefore the name of the place is called Gilgal unto this day.
>
> Joshua 5:2–9 (KJV)

After Joshua made the people be circumcised, the Lord said He had now "rolled away" (meaning commit and remove) the reproach of Egypt from off you. Gilgal means "a rolling."

The word reproach in Strong's Concordance means contumely, disgrace, and the pudenda:–rebuke, reproach (-fully), shame.[7]

The reproach of Egypt means that place of disgrace, or fall from grace. To fall from the grace of God (i.e., taking control of our own lives, doing it "our way") brings reproach upon us. We dis His grace and bring disgrace.

Contumely means resisting authority; pudenda means shame. Resisting His authority will ultimately bring shame upon us. If you are feeling shame, perhaps you have been resisting His authority and doing things your own way. Get realigned to His purposes and He will restore the years the locusts have eaten (Joel 2:12–27).

The Israelites didn't circumcise their children when they were in the wilderness. They were resisting the authority of God, and his representative Moses. The reproach (disgrace) of Egypt came upon them.

If you don't allow your heart to be circumcised, you will be resisting God and not be able to resist the temptations of the world, as James 4:7 tells us to submit to God first, then resist the devil and he will flee from you.

Through Abraham's seed, the "chosen" people came forth, chosen by God to be blessed by His covenant. Circumcision is a token of the covenant.

> This is my covenant, which ye shall keep, between me and you and thy seed after thee; Every man child among you shall be circumcised. And ye shall circumcise the flesh of your foreskin; and it shall be a token of the covenant betwixt me and you. And he that is eight days old shall be circumcised among you, every man child in your generations, he that is born in the house, or bought with money of any stranger, which is not of thy seed. He that is born in thy house, and he that is bought with thy money, must need be circumcised: and my covenant shall be in your flesh for an everlasting covenant.
>
> Genesis 17:10–13 (KJV)

> And it shall come to pass, when all these things are come upon thee, the blessing and the curse, which I have set

before thee, and thou shalt call them to mind among all the nations, whither the Lord thy God hath driven thee, And shalt return unto the Lord thy God, and shalt obey his voice according to all that I command thee this day, thou and thy children, with all thine heart, and with all thy soul; That then the Lord thy God will turn thy captivity, and have compassion upon thee, and will return and gather thee from all the nations, whither the Lord thy God hath scattered thee. If any of thine be driven out unto the outmost parts of heaven, from thence will the Lord thy God gather thee, and from thence will he fetch thee: And the Lord thy God will bring thee into the land which thy fathers possessed, and thou shalt possess it; and he will do thee good, and multiply thee above thy fathers. And the Lord thy God will circumcise thine heart, and the heart of thy seed, to love the Lord thy God with all thine heart, and with all thy soul, that thou mayest live.

Deuteronomy 30:1–6 (KJV)

The blessing and the curse…if you do what He says, He will circumcise your heart and your descendants' hearts, to love Him with all your heart and soul, that you may live, if you return and obey His voice.

God was going to kill Moses because he didn't circumcise his son. Without circumcision, an Israelite is cut off from the covenant. The same with us; without circumcision of our heart, we are cut off from our covenant with God. The first commandment (and the greatest, Jesus tells us), is to love the Lord your God with all your heart, soul, and mind.

Zipporah, Moses's wife, circumcised their son so that Moses wouldn't be destroyed.

And it came to pass by the way in the inn, that the Lord met him, and sought to kill him. Then Zipporah took a sharp stone, and cut off the foreskin of her son, and cast it at his feet, and said, Surely a bloody husband art thou to me. So he let him go: then she said, A bloody husband thou art, because of the circumcision.

Exodus 4:24–26 (KJV)

Jesus's blood is the new covenant, the better covenant. The circumcision that we are required to have is that of separation of our flesh and spirit, or heart, according to Paul.

> For he is not a Jew, which is one outwardly; neither is that circumcision, which is outward in the flesh: But he is a Jew, which is one inwardly; and circumcision is that of the heart, in the spirit, and not in the letter; whose praise is not of men, but of God.

Romans 2:28–29 (KJV)

> Beware lest any man spoil you through philosophy and vain deceit, after the tradition of men, after the rudiments of the world, and not after Christ. For in him dwelleth all the fullness of the Godhead bodily. And ye are complete in him, which is the head of all principality and power: In whom also ye are circumcised with the circumcision made without hands, in putting off the body of the sins of the flesh by the circumcision of Christ: Buried with him in baptism, wherein also ye are risen with him through the faith of the operation of God, who hath raised him from the dead. And you, being dead in your sins and the uncircumcision of your flesh, hath he quickened together with him, having forgiven you all trespasses;

Colossians 2:8–13 (KJV)

> For we are the circumcision, which worship God in the spirit, and rejoice in Christ Jesus, and have no confidence in the flesh.

Philippians 3:3 (KJV)

It is our flesh that causes us to murmur against God. We are to circumcise our flesh so that we can live by our spirit. We have a body, and in it the fleshly desires, but we are a spirit, created in the image of God originally, and now reborn with the life of Christ in us. Before we did not have a choice, the Adamic nature in us ruled. Now we have a choice, because Christ is in us, yet we have a body that will be serving someone. Whom shall we serve today?

In Exodus 32, as Moses was on Mount Sinai seeking God, the people became impatient and created their own god. In their impatience, they spoke rashly, provoking one another to disobedience, which led to their idolatrous actions. Isn't that what we do when we become impatient, waiting for God? We don't speak in faith, but unbelief, provoking others to disobedience also.

Colossians 3 speaks of the wrath of God, for the "things sake." We are to render dead the works done in the flesh.

> Mortify therefore your members which are upon the earth; fornication, uncleanness, inordinate affection, evil concupiscence, and covetousness, which is idolatry: For which things' sake the wrath of God cometh on the children of disobedience: But now ye also put off all these; anger, wrath, malice, blasphemy, filthy communication out of your mouth.
>
> Colossians 3:5–6, 8 (KJV)

The works in the flesh bring the wrath of God upon them (Rom. 1:18-20). God is holy and He is just. His very being is just, justice pours forth from Him, and if our works are those of the flesh, they will be destroyed. We have the Spirit of Christ in us, the Spirit of Holiness, warring against the spirit of the world that works in our fleshly desires and actions. The lust of the eyes, the lust of the flesh, and the pride of life (1 John 2:16) are of the spirit of the world. God is holy, and His presence destroys evil. When we perform evil works, His holy presence in us brings wrath upon the evil works we have done. Technically, we are bringing judgment and wrath upon ourselves! Yet we are assured in 1 John 1:9 that if we confess our sins, He is faithful and just to forgive us our sins, and to cleanse us from all unrighteousness.

## Shocking: We Are Creating Patterns of Good or Evil; We Exercise Our Heart to Love God or Self

God will judge our disobedience. His nature is holy, and holiness shines its light, showing disobedience. It is His nature in us that judges us. Then we cry out, and He delivers us (Judg. 2:18–3:7). We can go along in this pattern forever, or we can see with our spiritual eyes and choose to obey God, to follow Him and create a new pattern for our lives. God's best for us is not to be bridled as a horse and led along with a bit, but to walk in obedience until such time that His righteousness in us has built a new man.

> I will instruct thee and teach thee in the way which thou shalt go: I will guide thee with mine eye. Be ye not as the horse, or as the mule, which have no understanding: whose mouth must be held in with bit and bridle, lest they come near unto thee.
>
> Psalms 32:8–9 (KJV)

What does it mean to be guided by God's eye? If you watch a man and woman who have been married for a length of time, you can see that their communication is so finely attuned that one can give the slightest eye movement to another at a dinner party, and the other knows that it is time to leave. A mother who has trained her child to be attuned to her will be able to correct a behavior by a stern look.

To be guided by God's eye is to know God and His ways so intimately that you see as He sees. This new man walks in freedom because his senses have been exercised to discern between good and evil; having chosen good consistently, the patterns of Christ-likeness have taken hold and the choices made are those

Christ makes. We have learned to see through the eyes of the Spirit; we are seeing as He sees, therefore making good choices. God wants us so closely attuned that He can direct us by the eye of the Holy Spirit, the slightest impression we recognize because our senses have been exercised to that end.

> Of whom we have many things to say, and hard to be uttered, seeing ye are dull of hearing. For when for the time ye ought to be teachers, ye have need that one teach you again which be the first principles of the oracles of God; and are become such as have need of milk, and not of strong meat. For every one that useth milk is unskilful in the word of righteousness: for he is a babe. But strong meat belongeth to them that are of full age, even those who by reason of use have their senses exercised to discern both good and evil.
>
> Hebrews 5:11-14 (KJV)

> Now no chastening for the present seemeth to be joyous, but grievous: nevertheless afterward it yieldeth the peaceable fruit of righteousness unto them which are exercised thereby.
>
> Hebrews 12:11 (KJV)

> Having eyes full of adultery, and that cannot cease from sin; beguiling unstable souls: an heart they have exercised with covetous practices; cursed children:
>
> 2 Peter 2:14 (KJV)

We can see by these verses that God chastens us so that we will learn from it and begin to live a righteous life. We can use our natural senses to discern spiritually, and exercise our heart toward good or evil by what we practice in our lives. Conversely, we can exercise our hearts toward evil by continually pleasing our flesh, coveting constantly what we set before our eyes. The eye is never satisfied (Prov. 27:20); therefore, we can set our eyes on the fleshly desires or on the riches of Christ. Given that the eye is never satisfied, how much better to look upon Christ and exercise our heart to desire more of Him!

As we continue to exercise our senses to discern spiritually, we will become acutely aware of the Holy Spirit's guidance, and in that place of great discernment it is God's very nature in us that judges us moment by moment. Continued practice of obedience creates in us an acute sensitivity to the slightest impression of the Holy Spirit so that we can know confidently that we are in His will; we will not have His peace if we are not.

Looking at the verses in Hebrews again, we can see that there is an equally shocking reality, that one may have received great revelation at one time and later become dull of hearing and no longer able to receive revelation. There is a danger of becoming complacent, where we stop exercising our spiritual senses. There is no "arriving" and settling in His Kingdom. He always wants us to come up higher. Hebrews 5:13 says that some are unskillful in the word of righteousness. This can be a hard saying to one who once "knew something" and thought that was enough. We have to hear the word, receive it and keep it in our hearts. We also have to keep a guard on our heart and thoughts to ensure that we are in faith and that our direction is still towards God.

Paul warns those who have been in this awhile (he says those who by now should be teachers) against hardening of the heart which leads to needing to be fed milk again, rather than able to eat meat. Babies drink milk, they lay there like a lump and don't really need much energy. Milk just goes right through them and those around them take care of all their needs. When they get older and start moving they need meat. The protein in meat gets stored in the muscles for use later. Meat is a lot harder to digest. The body has to work harder to digest it, but it gains much energy from it.

This is true for the Word of God in our lives, and our need to exercise our heart towards the truth we receive from the Word, and to exercise our heart to refuse the lies that we hear from the world, the devil or our own soulish or fleshly desires. There is a great responsibility if we are to receive further revelation. We must gird up the loins of our mind to discern between good and evil. The enemy will come in and we will need to have exercised thought towards the Word so that we can recognize the lies. Thank God for the Holy Spirit, our Helper! He is always reminding us of Truth and comforting us when we mess up, ready to reveal Christ to us in that place of need!

## Shocking: As We Treat God, So We Receive from Him through the Hands of Others

He is trying to show us our heart toward Him.

> But Jeshurun waxed fat, and kicked: thou art waxen fat, thou art grown thick, thou art covered with fatness; then he forsook God which made him, and lightly esteemed the Rock of his salvation. They provoked him to jealousy with strange gods, with abominations provoked they him to anger. They sacrificed unto devils, not to God; to gods whom they knew not, to new gods that came newly up, whom your fathers feared not. Of the Rock that begat thee thou art unmindful, and hast forgotten God that formed thee. And when the LORD saw it, he abhorred them, because of the provoking of his sons, and of his daughters. And he said, I will hide my face from them, I will see what their end shall be: for they are a very forward generation, children in whom is no faith. They have moved me to jealousy with that which is not God; they have provoked me to anger with their vanities: and I will move them to jealousy with those which are not a people; I will provoke them to anger with a foolish nation. For a fire is kindled in mine anger, and shall burn unto the lowest hell, and

shall consume the earth with her increase, and set on fire the foundations of the mountains. I will heap mischiefs upon them; I will spend mine arrows upon them. They shall be burnt with hunger, and devoured with burning heat, and with bitter destruction: I will also send the teeth of beasts upon them, with the poison of serpents of the dust. The sword without, and terror within, shall destroy both the young man and the virgin, the suckling also with the man of gray hairs. I said, I would scatter them into corners, I would make the remembrance of them to cease from among men: Were it not that I feared the wrath of the enemy, lest their adversaries should behave themselves strangely, and lest they should say, Our hand is high, and the LORD hath not done all this. For they are a nation void of counsel, neither is there any understanding in them. O that they were wise, that they understood this, that they would consider their latter end!

Deuteronomy 32:15–29 (KJV)

If we forsake God and serve the devil, we receive evil. God's holiness responds to evil by destroying it. It isn't necessarily a punishment; He wants us to be filled with good. Evil has to be seen as evil before we are willing to take an axe to the root of it. God's creative power in us will magnify whatever it is until we see it.

Israel's treatment of God brought the same treatment back on them—when they thought they could hide from God, He hid from them. When they provoked Him to jealousy, He provoked them. When they caused Him to burn with anger, He brought burning to them—burning of hunger and heat or destruction.

See what is going on in your life and consider, where is your heart toward God? How are others treating you? As examples, are the people in your life jealous, angry or bitter? Do you feel ignored? Is it possible that they are reflecting your heart toward God? We know there is persecution to those living for Christ; that is not what I'm speaking of here. I'm speaking of the devils you are fighting. Those devils may be God's tool of correction to bring you into a higher place after you overcome the evil that has been allowed in (Is. 57:15-21). Food for thought...

God's righteous judgments are like shock treatments to us—they jolt us back to reality. We wander around, dazed by the material world, numb to all but our own senses and desires, and He desires us to be awake and alert to Him, sensitive to His leading. When we see truth, it is the proverbial lightbulb going off. His judgments awaken us to His holiness and righteousness. The blessings of God, especially when we don't deserve it (not that we ever do) awaken us to His love and mercy.

## Shocking: Who We Love and Serve Brings the Reward of the Same

Christ is eternal and life giving. When we love the world and the things in it, death is produced. If we love the world, destruction comes because love destroys evil. If God, who is love, allowed evil to continue rampantly, evil would destroy everything. It is out of love that God must destroy evil. If you love the world, you will receive destruction; if you love and serve God, you will receive life and blessing.

Who do you really love? The temptation of satanic pride is ever present.

> Beware that thou forget not the LORD thy God, in not keeping his commandments, and his judgments, and his statutes, which I command thee this day: Lest when thou hast eaten and art full, and hast built goodly houses, and dwelt therein; And when thy herds and thy flocks multiply, and thy silver and thy gold is multiplied, and all that thou hast is multiplied; Then thine heart be lifted up, and thou forget the LORD thy God, which brought thee forth out of the land of Egypt, from the house of bondage; Who led thee through that great and terrible wilderness, wherein were fiery serpents, and scorpions, and drought, where there was no water; who brought thee forth water out of the rock of flint; Who fed thee in the wilderness with manna, which thy fathers knew not, that he might humble

thee, and that he might prove thee, to do thee good at thy latter end; And thou say in thine heart, My power and the might of mine hand hath gotten me this wealth. But thou shalt remember the LORD thy God: for it is he that giveth thee power to get wealth, that he may establish his covenant which he sware unto thy fathers, as it is this day.

Deuteronomy 8:11–18 (KJV)

God will destroy your pride to humble you so that you can receive blessing in the end.

And it will be, if you will listen carefully to My commandments which I command you today, to love Jehovah your God and to serve Him with all your heart and with all your soul, I will give the rain of your land in its due season, the first rain and the latter rain, that you may gather in your grain and your wine and your oil. And I will send grass in your fields for your cattle so that you may eat and be full. Take heed to yourselves that your heart may not be deceived, and you turn aside and serve other gods, and worship them, and Jehovah's wrath be kindled against you, and He shut up the heavens so that there will be no rain, and so that the land will not yield her fruit, and you perish quickly from off the good land which Jehovah gives you.

Deuteronomy 11:13–17 (NKJV)

His Ways include the freedom to choose. God enables us to choose Him, through His grace. Yes, we have the inherent predisposition to sin handed down to us by generations before, from the beginning, when Adam and Eve sinned—they chose to disobey and all future generations now have that predisposition in our souls. We are created as souls with creative power; that is how we are made "in His image." What are we creating? Good or evil? By eating of the tree of the knowledge of good and evil, we now have to choose. We have fallen into the drama of the fight between good and evil. Prior to the fall, we lived in goodness only. When

Eve gave weight to the serpent's tempting words, she doubted what God said, and so do we when we give weight to lies. Prior to doubting God, we were completely and utterly in His image only, naive if you will to the reality of the war, but innocent as children who rely totally on their parents for everything they need. It is interesting to consider that if we are made in God's image, does He have the ability, or choice, to be anything but good? No, He is not evil. He is all-seeing and all-knowing, and He is always looking forward to the end whereby all of creation is reconciled to Himself. Everything He does is good because it is done with the intent to bring about His plan, which is good. It may look evil to us, and He even uses evil to bring His purposes to pass (see Isa. 45:7; Job 2:10). When we choose evil, God will use it to bring us back to Him. When we are in disobedience, we bring evil. Evil is an instrument used to destroy the evil in us so that we can repent and turn to good (see Lam. 3:37–40).

We are made in His image; note that He says let us make man in our image—Father, Son and Holy Spirit. He warns us not to make graven images for ourselves after our likeness. How often we try and build a persona that works in the world, a likeness that is a phantom image of who God has created us to be. And as we gaze upon the falseness, we begin to worship it because it is our craven heart's desire of what we perceive as beautiful, successful or even religious.

God tells us not to eat of the tree of the knowledge of good and evil. We are made in His likeness. We have the ability to create and He has given us dominion. If we eat of the tree of good and evil, we may not make the right choices.

In this instance in Genesis, the word knowledge in Strong's Concordance means to ascertain by seeing.[8] "Seeing," as opposed to trusting God and listening to His voice, being one with Him; seeing good and evil as opposed to innocently living in trust and reliance on Him.

The account in Genesis tells us that the serpent was more sub-til. Subtil in Strong's Concordance is the only instance of this word. It means cunning, usually in a bad sense, crafty and pru-dent; the root is a word that means to be (or make) bare.[9]

Now that we are "seeing" good and evil, we have a moral responsi-bility to do good. After we "see" by our first transgression (sin always inherent in our predisposition but not activated until we make con-scious choice), we feel condemnation and guilt. This perpetuates the cycle because we "know" we have sinned and try to cover it up (what-ever fig leaves we can find), to no avail. We recognize we are separated from God because we believed a lie about Him. Believing the lie was the error that caused the sin to take place. The serpent was, and is, cunning—crafty, subtle. Rest assured, he will never be obvious in the temptations he presents to us. How much better off we would be to keep in the forefront of our minds and hearts that God is good and His Word is forever true.

## *Shocking: The Issues in Our Life Arise from Our Heart*

Our murmurings bring the wrath of God (1 Corinthians 10:10; Numbers 14:2-20). God has given us creative ability; we are made in His image and He has given us dominion, a place of authority over creation. What do we do with it? Our words have creative power, and what we speak creates life or death (Proverbs 18:21). God is the creative force. We are co-creating with Him. If we speak forth words of death, the creative force in our words creates the result—and we see it as the wrath of God. Yet the words themselves are only a reflection of what is in our heart. God's word says to keep your heart with all diligence, for out of it spring forth the issues of life (Prov. 4:23).

According to Strong's Concordance, the word issues in this scripture means exit, that geographical boundary, or (figuratively) deliverance, borders, going forth, issues, outgoings.[10]

Our heart generates words that create the existing boundaries, the borders of our existence in life, or our deliverance out of these boundaries into His spiritual kingdom on this earth! Thank God for His grace and mercy that people don't drop dead right away from words of hate that have been spoken. Yet the old adage "sticks and stones will break your bones, but words will never hurt you" is a lie. Those words go into your soul and penetrate your heart; even if your mind knows it isn't true, there is a piercing that takes place, and it takes the healing power of love to overcome the wound. Unfortunately, over time, we tend to become desensitized to it; we harden our hearts to a certain extent and don't let anyone in. When my husband and I were first married, we were joking around, kiddingly casting some jibes here and there. I felt dirtied immediately, and we talked about it and agreed that we would not do that. It created an atmosphere of sullying the precious life that God has given; it was dishonoring. Say something enough and you begin to believe it.

The Holy Spirit hovered over the deep when the earth was without form and void (chaos), then God spoke. I believe that we need to allow the Holy Spirit in us to hover over a situation before we speak, to ensure that we are speaking life and not death. Let Him show us what is in our hearts, then choose life. We exercise our hearts toward good or evil (Hebrews 5:14 and 2 Peter 2:14). We create patterns and pathways. Our heart listens to our words, as well as others' words. How much different would our worlds be if we only spoke words of empowerment, life, and love? What if we truly believed that our words could make a difference in others' lives? They do. Try it. Test it. Prove it.

The reality in our Christian walk is that God is very gracious and merciful, yet He loves us enough to work with us and grow us up, that we will fulfill His purposes. Only in the fulfillment of His purpose for which we were created will we find true joy and satisfaction. When we reach a level of maturity, God begins to show us the effects of our words on others and ourselves.

God has always spoken to the end that those in darkness will come to the light and His correction for direction. Human nature wants to rely on our own strength—this is due to the fall, to pride, agreeing with the enemy that God is trying to hold us back from fulfilling our desires, implying that He is not good, seducing us to the desire to be our own gods. This is the lie inherent in all temptation—having our own way will be better; justifying our fleshly intentions with reasoning that is carnal—sense and reason without the Holy Spirit. Our flesh will always want its own way, and guaranteed it will not be for our good. Just think of any area of indulgence—what is the end of it, taken to its conclusion.... obesity, addiction, poverty, sexual disease.

God corrects so that we will turn and follow His direction, because He loves us and knows the end from the beginning. He knows the direction we need to go to find true fulfillment. He creates our circumstances—the fruit of our lips (Isaiah 57:19) —so that we can see what is in our hearts and turn to Him for help and healing.

# SHOCKING: THE REALITY THAT WORDS MATTER

## *Shocking: God Keeps His Word; Truth and Consequences*

Thou shalt not make unto thee any graven image, or any likeness of any thing that is in heaven above, or that is in the earth beneath, or that is in the water under the earth: Thou shalt not bow down thyself to them, nor serve them: for I the Lord thy God am a jealous God, visiting the iniquity of the fathers upon the children unto the third and fourth generation of them that hate me;

Exodus 20:4–5 (KJV)

And the people stood afar off, and Moses drew near unto the thick darkness where God was. And the Lord said unto Moses, Thus thou shalt say unto the children of Israel, Ye have seen that I have talked with you from heaven. Ye shall not make with me gods of silver, neither shall ye make unto you gods of gold.

Exodus 20:21–23 (KJV)

And when the people saw that Moses delayed to come down out of the mount, the people gathered themselves together unto Aaron, and said unto him, Up, make us gods, which shall go before us; for as for this Moses, the man that brought us up out of the land of Egypt, we wot not what is become of him. And Aaron said unto them, Break off the golden earrings, which are in the ears of your wives, of your sons, and of your daughters, and bring them unto me. And all the people break off the golden earrings which were in their ears, and brought them unto

Aaron. And he received them at their hand, and fashioned it with a graving tool, after he had made it a molten calf: and they said, These be thy gods, O Israel, which brought thee up out of the land of Egypt. And when Aaron saw it, he built an altar before it; and Aaron made proclamation, and said, To morrow is a feast to the LORD. And they rose up early on the morrow, and offered burnt offerings, and brought peace offerings; and the people sat down to eat and to drink, and rose up to play. And the LORD said unto Moses, Go, get thee down; for thy people, which thou broughtest out of the land of Egypt, have corrupted themselves: They have turned aside quickly out of the way which I commanded them: they have made them a molten calf, and have worshipped it, and have sacrificed thereunto, and said, These be thy gods, O Israel, which have brought thee up out of the land of Egypt. And the LORD said unto Moses, I have seen this people, and, behold, it is a stiff-necked people: Now therefore let me alone, that my wrath may wax hot against them, and that I may consume them: and I will make of thee a great nation.

Exodus 32:1–10 (KJV)

God was going to make a new nation of people. He'd had enough of their rebellion and disobedience. What was Moses's reaction? He interceded on their behalf, reasoning to God that if He destroyed the people, then the Egyptians would say He was an evil god.

And Moses besought the LORD his God, and said, LORD, why doth thy wrath wax hot against thy people, which thou hast brought forth out of the land of Egypt with great power, and with a mighty hand? Wherefore should the Egyptians speak, and say, For mischief did he bring them out, to slay them in the mountains, and to consume them from the face of the earth? Turn from thy fierce wrath, and repent of this evil against thy people. Remember Abraham, Isaac, and Israel, thy servants, to whom thou swarest by thine own self, and saidst unto them, I will multiply your seed as the stars of heaven, and all this land that I have spoken of will I give unto your seed, and they shall inherit it forever. And the LORD repented of the evil which he thought to do unto his people.

Exodus 32:11–14

God gave them another chance to turn from their ways.

And Moses turned, and went down from the mount, and the two tables of the testimony were in his hand: the tables were written on both their sides; on the one side and on the other were they written. And the tables were the work of God, and the writing was the writing of God, graven upon the tables. And when Joshua heard the noise of the people as they shouted, he said unto Moses, There is a noise of war in the camp. And he said, It is not the voice of them that shout for mastery, neither is it the voice of them that cry for being overcome: but the noise of them that sing do I hear. And it came to pass, as soon as he came nigh unto the camp, that he saw the calf, and the dancing: and Moses' anger waxed hot, and he cast the tables out of his hands, and break them beneath the mount. And he took the calf which they had made, and burnt it in the fire, and ground it to powder, and strawed it upon the water, and made the children of Israel drink of it. And Moses said unto Aaron, What did this people unto thee, that thou hast brought so great a sin upon them? And Aaron said, Let not the anger of my lord wax hot: thou knowest the people, that they are set on mischief. For they said unto me, Make us gods, which shall go before us: for as for this Moses, the man that brought us up out of the land of Egypt, we wot not what is become of him. And I said unto them, Whosoever hath any gold, let them break it off. So they gave it me: then I cast it into the fire, and there came out this calf. And when Moses saw that the people were naked; (for Aaron had made them naked unto their shame among their enemies:

Exodus 32:15–25 (KJV)

This is significant. Although Aaron gave them what they wanted, he recognized the evil and the lack of covering they now had by turning to worthless idols; the removal of their clothing signifies their lack of covering. It also signifies that Aaron recognized their evil desires and the reality of a harsh consequence/ punishment.

> Then Moses stood in the gate of the camp, and said, Who is on the LORD's side? let him come unto me. And all the sons of Levi gathered themselves together unto him. And he said unto them, Thus saith the LORD God of Israel, Put every man his sword by his side, and go in and out from gate to gate throughout the camp, and slay every man his brother, and every man his companion, and every man his neighbour. And the children of Levi did according to the word of Moses: and there fell of the people that day about three thousand men. For Moses had said, Consecrate yourselves to day to the LORD, even every man upon his son, and upon his brother; that he may bestow upon you a blessing this day. And it came to pass on the morrow, that Moses said unto the people, Ye have sinned a great sin: and now I will go up unto the LORD; peradventure I shall make an atonement for your sin. And Moses returned unto the LORD, and said, Oh, this people have sinned a great sin, and have made them gods of gold. Yet now, if thou wilt forgive their sin—; and if not, blot me, I pray thee, out of thy book which thou hast written. And the LORD said unto Moses, Whosoever hath sinned against me, him will I blot out of my book. Therefore now go, lead the people unto the place of which I have spoken unto thee: behold, mine Angel shall go before thee: nevertheless in the day when I visit I will visit their sin upon them. And the LORD plagued the people, because they made the calf, which Aaron made.
>
> Exodus 32:26–35

The Lord "plagued" the people. God had told them emphatically not to make other gods of gold or silver. They had said this golden calf was their god, as was with the Egyptians. God plagued the Egyptians.

God is creative and His power is dunamis, where we get the word dynamite. Yet His power is always working for His purposes—to establish His kingdom and destroy evil. If we are linked to evil, His power will be working to destroy that evil. Thank God for His mercy. He may destroy our idols and those things we are set on that are contrary to Life, so that we may be saved.

> To deliver such a one unto Satan for the destruction of the flesh, that the spirit may be saved in the day of the Lord Jesus.
>
> 1 Corinthians 5:5 (KJV)

> Perhaps the people will listen and give up their evil ways. If they do, then I will change my mind about the destruction I plan to bring on them for all their wicked deeds.
>
> Jeremiah 26:3 (CEV)

The purpose of plagues or any other type of punishment is to show God's power and fame, because He is always working to have his creation reconciled to Himself. He wants to show us good and bless us! He exhorts in Deuteronomy 5:29 (KJV), "O that there were such an heart in them, that they would fear me, and keep all my commandments always, that it might be well with them, and with their children forever!"

The three thousand were those that did not turn back to the Lord God when He gave them their second chance. To those who did return to the Lord, their ten times of provoking Him would meet its due reward by their not entering the Promised Land. They were saved from death but did not receive the promises in this life. This, then, is the result for Christians in this life who are not obedient; salvation unto eternal life is granted, but there is no overcoming life, no receiving His great and precious promises for abundant spiritual life in this world. For to receive and walk in abundant spiritual life, you have to believe Him regardless of what the circumstances shout.

Check yourself. Are there plagues in your life? If the enemy is working, God is allowing it—He creates the tools for the enemy to use (Isaiah 54:16-17), for His purposes to come forth. Our flesh thinks we are being punished, or that good is being withheld from us. Remember, Satan's ploy was to deceive Eve into thinking God was withholding from her (Genesis, chapter 3).

## *Shocking: You Have What You Say*

> For truly I say to you that whoever shall say to this mountain, Be moved and be cast into the sea, and shall not doubt in his heart, but shall believe that what he said shall occur, he shall have whatever he said.
>
> Mark 11:23 (NKJV)

As we learned, the people did not get to enter into the Promised Land because of fear and unbelief. However, we must also note that the words that they spoke in fear and unbelief would be done unto them.

> And all the congregation lifted up their voice and cried. And the people wept that night. And all the sons of Israel murmured against Moses and against Aaron. And the whole congregation said to them, Oh that we had died in the land of Egypt! Or, Oh that we had died in the wilderness! And why has Jehovah brought us into this land to fall by the sword, so that our wives and our sons should be a prey? Would it not be better for us to return to Egypt? And they said to one another, Let us make a leader, and let us return to Egypt.
>
> Numbers 14:1-4 (NKJV)

Say to them, As I live, says Jehovah, as you have spoken in My ears, so I will do to you. Your dead bodies shall fall in this wilderness, and all that were numbered of you, according to your whole number, from twenty years old and upward, who have murmured against Me, you shall certainly not come into the land which I swore to make you live in, except Caleb the son of Jephunneh, and Joshua the son of Nun. But your little ones, which you said should be a prey, I will bring them in and they shall know the land which you have despised. But as for you, your bodies shall fall in this wilderness. And your sons shall feed in the wilderness forty years and bear your fornications, until your dead bodies have wasted in the wilderness. According to the number of the days in which you searched the land, forty days, each day for a year you shall bear your iniquities, forty years; and you shall know My alienation. I Jehovah have spoken; I will surely do it to all this evil congregation who are gathered together against Me. They shall be destroyed in this wilderness, and there they shall die.

Numbers 14:28–35 (NKJV)

David speaks to us of this wisdom in Psalms 18:25–26 (NKJV), "With the merciful, You will show Yourself merciful; with an upright man You will show Yourself upright; with the pure You will show Yourself pure; and with the crooked You will show Yourself perverse."

The commandment "Thou shall not take the name of the Lord thy God in vain; for the Lord will not hold him guiltless that taketh His name in vain" (Ex. 20:7 KJV), when broken down into the actual Hebrew language, is very interesting. In this instance, vain according to Strong's Concordance, means desolating, evil, destructive (ruin or guide); figuratively, idolatry or uselessness.[11]

When we attribute God's name (name means authority and character) to evil, destruction or uselessness, we are taking His name in vain. When we think that God's intent toward us is evil, or that He doesn't care about us, we are taking His name in vain!

How important it is to observe and recognize what is the inherent belief behind our thoughts? If I am fearful or fretting about an upcoming event in my life, what does that say I believe? Do I believe that God is sovereign, that He does provide, that He is working on my behalf? Or do I believe that He will not provide, that He will leave me desolate and without resources to succeed? We must guard our thoughts, for out of our heart (our belief system, where our thoughts originate) proceed the issues of life. To guard our thoughts, we must examine them. To examine them, we must take the time to look. Often when we are fretting, we are meditating over and over again on the problem and confessing lies over and over again, such as This is terrible; This is going to kill me; I can't handle this; We'll never get out of debt; I'm always getting sick; I don't know what to do; This will never change; We'll always be broke, sick, lonely, struggling, unhappy, depressed. What about confessing God's words instead: "Grace and mercy shall follow me all the days of my life; He will never leave me or forsake me; By His stripes I am healed; The Lord keeps covenant to a thousand generations for those who love Him and keep His commandments; My God shall supply all my needs according to His riches in glory by Christ Jesus."

> My son, attend to my words; incline thine ear unto my sayings. Let them not depart from thine eyes; keep them in the midst of thine heart. For they are life unto those that find them, and health to all their flesh. Keep thy heart with all diligence; for out of it are the issues of life.
>
> Proverbs 4:20–23 (KJV)

> But knowing their thoughts, answering, Jesus said to them, Why do you reason in your hearts?
>
> Luke 5:22 (NKJV)

> For truly I say to you that whoever shall say to this moun-
> tain, Be moved and be cast into the sea, and shall not
> doubt in his heart, but shall believe that what he said shall
> occur, he shall have whatever he said.
>
> Mark 11:23 (NKJV)

Could it be possible that some of the "bad" things in your life
are the result of wrong beliefs and the things you have spoken?
Shocking if true....but is it shocking enough to have us begin to
examine our heart, as out of it flows the issues in our life. How
does it flow out of our heart? It becomes sin through the members
of our body—our mouth, our eyes, our hands and feet going in
the wrong direction. The tongue is a little member, but the Bible
says it directs the whole body (James 3:5–6). I've heard it said
and have to agree, "Check yourself before you wreck yourself."

## Shocking: God Keeps His Word—Obedience Brings Blessing

This may seem like a no-brainer, but like many things that we
assume we believe, it often pays to look a little deeper. Do we
believe that obedience brings blessing? In the fast-paced, micro-
wave-ready, remote-control changing society we live in, we
expect instant gratification. God's ways are not like ours. He usually doesn't bless us immediately but waits until He sees if we are
doing it to receive the blessing or because we believe that He is
true and worth following. There is a difference. A child who obeys
just to get a present learns to manipulate and control, because
there is an inherent bribery in the method. God is seeking relationship, and isn't it true that a child who loves their parent trusts
them and willingly does what they desire to please them, not for a
reward other than the pleasure of gaining the parent's acceptance.
We may know that our parents (and God) love us, and we long
for them to accept our actions and choices. When we are small,
our parents (if wise) will see the long-term result of our poor

choices and by loving us, punish our wrongdoing and reward our good choices. Thank goodness God is loving and wise, and orders our circumstances for our long-term benefit. The problem is that in our society, we take pride in being independent, wanting to be our own god and control our own destiny.

God's Word makes it very plain, especially in Deuteronomy, chapters 28–30, where the blessings and curses are laid out for us. If this, then that. God doesn't make it too difficult to figure out. So what usually happens when we don't see an immediate result to standing upon the Word of God? On some level we stop believing; we become discouraged and faithless and give up on His Word. If we took the time to identify our thoughts, they'd probably be something like, "Did God really say that to me, maybe it isn't for me?" Sound familiar? This was Satan tempting Eve, and it is the same old story today. I'd venture to say that we don't usually examine our thoughts because we've forgotten the Word; we've lost the glimmer of hope, now squelched down by our circumstances. Could it be that our circumstances are the tribulation spoken of "on account of the word" in Mark 4:14–17? Our circumstances may not be the great tribulation coming at the end of the age, but they are trouble enough for us in standing our ground and waiting for God to be glorified. "Many are the afflictions of the righteous, but the Lord delivers him out of them all" (Ps. 34:19 KJV). Do we believe? Speak it out! Confess it with our mouth so our ears hear until our hearts believe again!

After we're saved, Satan's plan is to render us ineffective in the kingdom—to not fulfill our destiny in Christ. God allows Satan's attacks, his bringing of doubt and discouragement. It is part of the process of the trying of His Word in us. His Word will not return void. It may take a while, as the areas of our soul that are in conflict and opposition to His truth need to be uprooted (Matt. 15:13), and our flesh is lazy and wants comfort. Our flesh will always be in opposition to the Spirit of God (Gal. 5:17). It isn't an overnight process, but the process can be shortened if we continue to believe, confessing truth over ourselves, seeking godly counsel, praying without ceasing, praising in the storm and, above all, standing in faith when we want to lie down in negativity. We are to rise up in our thoughts and not give in to the other voices, whether it is the voice of the devil, the world, or our own flesh.

Or perhaps we continue to believe but think we should take matters into our own hands and do the work for Him (as Abraham and Sarah, with Hagar), rather than standing on the Word and saying, "God is not a man that He should lie, neither the son of man that He should repent. Has He said, and shall He not do it? Or has He spoken, and shall He not make it good?" (Num. 23:19 NKJV).

The trying of the word is a process. "The words of the Lord are pure words: as silver tried in a furnace of earth, purified seven times" (Ps. 12:6 KJV). Jesus made it very plain in the parable of the sower that Satan will come immediately to try and steal the word out of our hearts, and that tribulation and persecution will come on account of the word.

> The sower soweth the word. And these are they by the way side, where the word is sown; but when they have heard, Satan cometh immediately, and taketh away the word that was sown in their hearts. And these are they likewise which are sown on stony ground; who, when they have heard the word, immediately receive it with gladness; And have no root in themselves, and so endure but for a time: afterward, when affliction or persecution ariseth for the word's sake, immediately they are offended.
>
> Mark 4:14–17 (KJV)

There will be, there must be, a trying process. This is where our faith is tested and tried and comes out as pure gold, and where we see our own efforts as rubbish. Blessing will come, but we must be patient, and this is where the rubber meets the road for most of us. Even Abraham, known as the father of our faith, took matters into his own (and Sarah's) hands when they got weary of waiting for the promise of a son. The result was tragic for them and for the world as Ishmael's generations continue to war with Isaac's. Yet this is God's plan for redemption. He shows us the folly of following the flesh, our own reasoning, and the stark difference between man's attempts at controlling his destiny and God's bountiful blessings when we walk in obedience to His words.

> Come now, and let us reason together, saith the LORD: though your sins be as scarlet, they shall be as white as snow; though they be red like crimson, they shall be as wool. If ye be willing and obedient, ye shall eat the good of the land: But if ye refuse and rebel, ye shall be devoured with the sword: for the mouth of the LORD hath spoken it.
>
> Isaiah 1:18–20 (KJV)

Interestingly, the word sword in the Hebrew language means drought, according to Strong's Concordance.[12] The truth is that everything we need is found in the riches in glory by Christ Jesus, according to Philippians 4:19. And in Colossians 1:16–17 (KJV) we read that "For by him were all things created, that are in heaven, and that are in earth, visible and invisible, whether they be thrones, or dominions, or principalities, or powers: all things were created by him, and for him: And he is before all things, and by him all things consist."

All that we have need of the Father knows and will provide when we seek first His kingdom and His righteousness (Matt. 6:33). All things created by Him are at His command; even the winds and seas obey Him (Mk. 4:41). Without Him, our lives are full of drought, dry and empty, a continual struggle of survival of the fittest.

James 4:2–3 says that we have not because we ask not, and when we do ask, we ask amiss, to satisfy it on our own lusts. God always looks at the heart. When we pray, are we seeking God's face and His will, or are we asking Him to bless our own little kingdom that we created for ourselves?

> Servants, obey in all things your masters according to the flesh; not with eyeservice, as menpleasers; but in singleness of heart, fearing God: And whatsoever ye do, do it heartily, as to the Lord, and not unto men; Knowing that of the Lord ye shall receive the reward of the inheritance: for ye serve the Lord Christ.
>
> Colossians 3:22–24 (KJV)

It is God's desire to give us the kingdom (Luke 12:32). What more could we possibly need or want than the kingdom of the Lord of Glory?

## Shocking: God Honors Vows Made with Our Lips, Even When We Have Forgotten Them

### ASA (WHICH MEANS PHYSICIAN)

> For the eyes of the LORD run to and fro throughout the whole earth, to shew himself strong in the behalf of them whose heart is perfect toward him. Herein thou hast done foolishly: therefore from henceforth thou shalt have wars.
>
> 2 Chronicles 16:9 (KJV)

In 2 Chronicles 14:1–3, and 1 Kings 15:12–13, we read that Asa reigned as king of Judah and did what was good and right in the eyes (sight) of the Lord (the Lord's eyes always searching to show Himself strong on behalf of one whose heart is perfect toward Him). We see that Asa

1. took away the altars of the foreign gods,

2. took away the high places,

3. broke down the images,

4. took away the sodomites,

5. cut down the groves (representing places fertility rituals were performed),

6. commanded Judah to seek the Lord God,
7. commanded Judah to obey the law and commandments.

As a result, the kingdom was quiet before him. During this time of quiet, they built and prospered. After a time, the Ethiopian army, twice their size, came against them. Asa called on the Lord, and the Lord smote them and prevailed.

> And Asa cried unto the LORD his God, and said, LORD, it is nothing with thee to help, whether with many, or with them that have no power: help us, O LORD our God; for we rest on thee, and in thy name we go against this multitude. O LORD, thou art our God; let not man prevail against thee. So the LORD smote the Ethiopians before Asa, and before Judah; and the Ethiopians fled. And Asa and the people that were with him pursued them unto Gerar: and the Ethiopians were overthrown, that they could not recover themselves; for they were destroyed before the LORD, and before his host; and they carried away very much spoil.
>
> 2 Chronicles 14:11–13 (KJV)

Azariah the Son of Oded prophesied to Asa that the Lord would be with him, and the nations of Judah and Benjamin, as long as they sought Him, but that if they forsook the Lord, He would forsake them. He recounted the history of Israel, comparing times they sought God to when they didn't, as an example (2 Chron. 15). Asa was encouraged, and in the fifteenth year of his reign, he put away all the idols in Judah and Benjamin, and all the cities they had taken, and renewed the altars of the Lord. He gathered all the people (many had fallen out of Israel to him when they saw the Lord was with him; Israel did not have all the high places removed). All those that came under Asa's reign during this time entered into covenant and sought the Lord with all their heart and soul.

So they gathered themselves together at Jerusalem in the third month, in the fifteenth year of the reign of Asa. And they offered unto the LORD the same time, of the spoil which they had brought, seven hundred oxen and seven thousand sheep. And they entered into a covenant to seek the LORD God of their fathers with all their heart and with all their soul; That whosoever would not seek the LORD God of Israel should be put to death, whether small or great, whether man or woman. And they sware unto the LORD with a loud voice, and with shouting, and with trumpets, and with cornets. And all Judah rejoiced at the oath: for they had sworn with all their heart, and sought him with their whole desire; and he was found of them: and the LORD gave them rest round about.

2 Chronicles 15:10–15 (KJV)

In Asa's thirty-sixth year of reign, King Baasham of Israel built the city of Ramah against Judah's border so that no more Israelites would go to Judah. In Strong's Concordance, we learn that Ramah means a height, as a seat of idolatry. [13]

Asa took gold and silver to King Ben-Hadad in Syria, asking that their alliance with Israel be broken so they would leave the area. Ben-Hadad agreed and went to war against Israel. Baasham left off building Ramah, and Asa carried away the stones and timber of Ramah and built Geba (meaning hillock) and Mizpah (meaning watchtower). Hanani the seer came and told Asa that because he relied on the king of Syria and not God, the host of the king of Syria escaped out of his hand. He reminded him of how God had delivered the Ethiopians unto his hand when he relied on God.

For the eyes of the LORD run to and fro throughout the whole earth, to shew himself strong in the behalf of them whose heart is perfect toward him. Herein thou hast done foolishly: therefore from henceforth thou shalt have wars. Then Asa was wroth with the seer, and put him in a prison house; for he was in a rage with him because of this thing. And Asa oppressed some of the people the same time. And, behold, the acts of Asa, first and last, lo, they are written in the book of the kings of Judah and Israel. And Asa in the thirty and ninth year of his reign was diseased in his feet, until his disease was exceeding great: yet in his disease he sought not to the LORD, but to the physicians. And Asa slept with his fathers, and died in the one and fortieth year of his reign.

2 Chronicles 16:9–13 (KJV)

God honors the vows we make with our lips, even when we forget. Asa had made a covenant that anyone not seeking the Lord would be put to death. He stopped seeking the Lord and sought the help of another nation. He then became ill and did not seek the Lord, but sought physicians instead. He died. His own words brought the curse of death upon himself.

This is shocking, heavy-duty. We (the church) are not to build alliances with the world to try and protect ourselves or build our house. The Lord is our strength, our defense. Romans 8:31 (KJV) asks, "If God be for us, who can be against us?" The church is not to be joined to the world (see 2 Cor. 6:17). The church is not to look to the world for answers. The church is not to be married to the world, but to the Lord (Rev. 21:9–11). We are to be separate, holy unto the Lord, seeking Him only, relying on Him only. He is our source and our strength. He is the creator of all things—how can we expect the "things" to save us, or to help us, or to guide us? God desires a people unto Himself. And He desires to bring His Kingdom to the earth—how will we do that but by relying on Him?

Do we believe? John 5:44 asks how can we, if we seek the praise and honor and glory that comes from man? If we are seeking praise and honor and glory from men, we are expecting something from them. Our hope is to be in God. Let's reason:

God creates all things. He influences all. He is sovereign, omnipotent, and omnipresent. To see otherwise is an illusion.

When we seek Him and obey Him, He (who holds all things) causes favor to come to us, for He desires to see Himself glorified. He, being glorified in us, draws all to Himself. His desire is that His creation be reconciled to Himself, that the god of this world be rendered powerless, for his (Satan's) power is only what we allow him to have. Jesus said the god of this world has nothing in Himself (John 14:30); if we abide in Him and allow Him to abide in us, there will be no influence that the god of this world can have in us. The victory has already taken place, at the cross. Jesus took away the keys of death and hell. Yet if we turn our hearts and minds away from Him, our will is no longer toward the Lord, and we turn to the world-system, giving the enemy a foothold in our lives.

When we give our lives to the Lord, He remembers. When we vow to follow Him, He honors this vow. We are held accountable for our words. This is a foundational truth that we cannot get away from or take lightly.

> When you shall vow a vow to Jehovah your God, you shall not wait to pay it, for Jehovah your God will surely require it of you, and it would be sin in you. But if you shall cease to vow, it shall be no sin in you. That which has gone out of your lips you shall keep and perform, even a free-will offering, according as you have vowed to Jehovah your God, which you have promised with your mouth.
>
> Deuteronomy 23:21–23 (NKJV)

> And Moses spoke to the heads of the tribes concerning the sons of Israel, saying, This is the thing which Jehovah has commanded: If a man vows a vow to Jehovah, or swears an oath to bind his soul with a bond, he shall not break his word. He shall do according to all that comes out of his mouth.
>
> Numbers 30:1–2 (NKJV)

## Shocking: What We Mutter Matters

Joshua recognized that it was imperative to speak and do exactly as God commanded. God gave Joshua authority because he believed and stood strong. Joshua succeeded where Moses failed. Moses failed to sanctify God before the people; he gave in to his anger and frustration. Joshua kept his eyes on the promises of God—to bring them into the Promised Land—but not only his eyes; he kept his mouth in line with the truth. God had told him that they would cross over; God told him the territory that was given to him. The word of the Lord to Joshua was to be strong and courageous because God was with him and would not ever fail him or forsake him. Joshua took hold of this and didn't let go.

And Joshua rose early in the morning; and they removed from Shittim, and came to Jordan, he and all the children of Israel, and lodged there before they passed over. And it came to pass after three days, that the officers went through the host; And they commanded the people, saying, When ye see the ark of the covenant of the LORD your God, and the priests the Levites bearing it, then ye shall remove from your place, and go after it. Yet there shall be a space between you and it, about two thousand cubits by measure: come not near unto it, that ye may know the way by which ye must go: for ye have not passed this way heretofore. (You may have to be a little removed from something to see with His eyes.) And Joshua said unto the people, Sanctify yourselves: for to morrow the LORD will do wonders among you. And Joshua spake unto the priests, saying, Take up the ark of the covenant, and pass over before the people. And they took up the ark of the covenant, and went before the people. And the LORD said unto Joshua, This day will I begin to magnify thee in the sight of all Israel, that they may know that, as I was with Moses, so I will be with thee. And thou shalt command the priests that bear the ark of the covenant, saying, When ye are come to the brink of the water of Jordan, ye shall stand still in Jordan. And Joshua said unto the children of Israel, Come hither, and hear the words of the LORD your God. And Joshua said, Hereby ye shall know that the living God is among you, and that he will without fail drive out from before you the Canaanites, and the Hittites, and the Hivites, and the Perizzites, and the Girgashites, and the Amorites, and the Jebusites. Behold, the ark of the covenant of the Lord of all the earth passeth over before you into Jordan. Now therefore take you twelve men out of the tribes of Israel, out of every tribe a man. And it shall come to pass, as soon as the soles of the feet of the priests that bear the ark of the LORD, the Lord of all the earth, shall rest in the waters of Jordan, that the waters of Jordan shall be cut off from the waters that come down from above; and they shall stand upon an heap. And it came to pass, when the people removed from their tents, to pass over Jordan, and the priests bearing the ark of the covenant before the people; And as they that bare the ark were come unto Jordan, and the feet of the priests that bare the ark were dipped in the brim of the water, (for Jordan overfloweth all his banks all the time of harvest,) That the waters which came down from above stood and rose up upon an heap very far from the city Adam, that is beside Zaretan: and those that came down toward the sea of the plain, even the salt sea, failed, and were cut off: and the people passed over right against Jericho. And the priests that bare the ark of the covenant of the LORD stood firm on dry ground in the midst of Jordan, and all the Israelites passed over on dry ground, until all the people were passed clean over Jordan.

Joshua 3:1–17 (KJV)

The Lord had told Joshua to meditate on the book of the law day and night; then he would make his way prosperous, and then he would have good success.

Only be thou strong and very courageous, that thou mayest observe to do according to all the law, which Moses
my servant commanded thee: turn not from it to the right
hand or to the left, that thou mayest prosper whithersoever
thou goest. This book of the law shall not depart out of thy
mouth; but thou shalt meditate therein day and night, that
thou mayest observe to do according to all that is written
therein: for then thou shalt make thy way prosperous, and
then thou shalt have good success. Have not I commanded
thee? Be strong and of a good courage; be not afraid, neither be thou dismayed: for the LORD thy God is with thee
whithersoever thou goest.

Joshua 1:7–9 (KJV)

In this instance, the word meditate in the Strong's Concordance
means to murmur; by implication to ponder:–imagine, meditate, mourn, mutter, roar, speak, study, talk, utter.[14] To murmur,
mutter, speak, talk, utter…Not just to think about. What was
Moses muttering?

He was repeating the complaints of the people, voicing his
frustration, and doubting God's ability. What do we mutter?
Have we forgotten God's promises to us? Are we repeating over
and over to ourselves problems and negativity? The Lord tells us
that He will never leave us or forsake us, that He has given us all
things that pertain to life and godliness, to be of good courage
because He has overcome the world (and therefore all that is in
the world). Yet we look at our circumstances and say, "I can't do
this, it is too hard, it will never change." We are to meditate on
the Word day and night, to stand upon and believe it, because it
is Truth.

Blessed is the man that walketh not in the counsel of the
ungodly, nor standeth in the way of sinners, nor sitteth
in the seat of the scornful. But his delight is in the law of
the LORD; and in his law doth he meditate day and night.
And he shall be like a tree planted by the rivers of water,

that bringeth forth his fruit in his season; his leaf also shall not wither; and whatsoever he doeth shall prosper. The ungodly are not so: but are like the chaff which the wind driveth away. Therefore the ungodly shall not stand in the judgment, nor sinners in the congregation of the righteous. For the LORD knoweth the way of the righteous: but the way of the ungodly shall perish.

Psalms 1:1–6 (KJV)

God put fear on all the surrounding nations through the separating of the Jordan waters so they could cross over. God is always showing Himself and looking for those who see and believe.

And Joshua said, Hereby ye shall know that the living God is among you, and that he will without fail drive out from before you the Canaanites, and the Hittites, and the Hivites, and the Perizzites, and the Girgashites, and the Amorites, and the Jebusites.

Joshua 3:10 (KJV)

God clearly lets us know that if we follow Him, he will drive out our enemies from before us. Note it says the enemies that are before us, not those among us. We are responsible in destroying the false gods among us because we have let them in. Truly, when we repent and trust wholly in Him, raising His name (character and authority), the enemy must flee. He is a bully and always looking for weaklings. When we are strong in the Lord and the power of His might, the enemy flees. We subdue our enemies by submitting to God (James 4:7). Yet when we are going forward into new territory, if we follow Him fully, He will drive out our enemies from before us...as we go forward. He will not drive them out if we don't begin walking forward. We will see the enemies before us; will we perceive them with natural eyes, wherein they look like giants, or will we perceive with spiritual eyes that He is much greater and stand upon His Word, knowing that He that is in us is greater than He that is in the world (1 John 4:4)?

Behold, the ark of the covenant of the Lord of all the earth passeth over before you into Jordan. Now therefore take you twelve men out of the tribes of Israel, out of every tribe a man. And it shall come to pass, as soon as the soles of the feet of the priests that bear the ark of the LORD, the Lord of all the earth, shall rest in the waters of Jordan, that the waters of Jordan shall be cut off from the waters that come down from above; and they shall stand upon an heap. And it came to pass, when the people removed from their tents, to pass over Jordan, and the priests bearing the ark of the covenant before the people; And as they that bare the ark were come unto Jordan, and the feet of the priests that bare the ark were dipped in the brim of the water, (for Jordan overfloweth all his banks all the time of harvest), That the waters which came down from above stood and rose up upon an heap very far from the city Adam, that is beside Zaretan: and those that came down toward the sea of the plain, even the salt sea, failed, and were cut off: and the people passed over right against Jericho. And the priests that bare the ark of the covenant of the LORD stood firm on dry ground in the midst of Jordan, and all the Israelites passed over on dry ground, until all the people were passed clean over Jordan.

Joshua 3:11–17 (KJV)

As soon as they crossed over, the Lord told Joshua to have each of the twelve men carry a large stone from the riverbed and place them where they were to lodge that night. These stones would be a memorial forever, to future generations, to instill in us the fear of the Lord.

And those twelve stones, which they took out of Jordan, did Joshua pitch in Gilgal. And he spake unto the children of Israel, saying, When your children shall ask their fathers in time to come, saying, What mean these stones? Then ye shall let your children know, saying, Israel came over this Jordan on dry land. For the LORD your God dried up the waters of Jordan from before you, until ye were passed over, as the LORD your God did to the Red Sea, which he dried up from before us, until we were gone over: That all the people of the earth might know the hand of the LORD, that it is mighty: that ye might fear the LORD your God for ever.

Joshua 4:20–24 (KJV)

God never does anything without a reason. The word stone in the Hebrew language means to build. Our faith is built on hearing. We need to hear the testimonies of the Lord's work in others and they need to hear ours. We need to teach our children what God has done in our lives and others, and teach them from the Bible so that they will hear and have faith in Him. Faith comes by hearing and hearing by the word of God. What is this word? Every word that He has spoken has the power to produce faith, when received in a heart that is open. He parted the waters of the Jordan River, as the Red Sea before. Think of the need in your life right now. Can you believe that He is able to provide the answer, perform the impossible? Is it harder to heal your body or influence someone's heart in your favor, or to dry up the waters of a mighty river, to part the sea? If you are in unbelief, bring to your remembrance all the times He came through in your hour of need. If you can't think of any, read the Word of God, the accounts throughout the Bible of God meeting needs, and let the Holy Spirit sprinkle your heart with faith so that you can believe God will do the same in your life. Remember, meditating on the Word means muttering to yourself. Speak louder than the voices of doubt and unbelief until your spirit man rises strongly over your soul.

## *Shocking: Our Words Create Our Reality*

Jesus said we will give an account of every idle word spoken, and by our words we will be justified or condemned.

> O generation of vipers, how can ye, being evil, speak good things? for out of the abundance of the heart the mouth speaketh. A good man out of the good treasure of the heart bringeth forth good things: and an evil man out of the evil treasure bringeth forth evil things. But I say unto you, That every idle word that men shall speak, they shall give account thereof in the day of judgment. For by thy words thou shalt be justified, and by thy words thou shalt be condemned.
>
> Matthew 12:34–37 (KJV)

In this scripture, the word treasure is the Greek word thesauros, and the root means a deposit, that is, wealth (literally or figuratively).

What words are you depositing in your heart? What you deposit will grow as wealth grows, with interest. When you think of the times you have said things that you regret, you say, "I didn't really mean it." The truth could be that a part of you did mean it, but there were other equally true things you could have said. One is true to the fleshly, sinful nature that demands your own way. The other words are true of the nature of Christ that is in you. Which are you feeding? When you are first in love, blind to the faults of your lover, what do you rehearse in your mind? The things you love about them. Now fast-forward to when you are hurt. What are you meditating on then? All the times they didn't meet your needs or disappointed you. In the spiritual realm, there is a battle raging at all times between God and Satan. We know that the thief comes to kill, steal, and destroy everything that belongs to God. God is love, desiring to bless us with good things. His Word is full of great and precious promises. Meditate on those things, things that are pure and lovely, things of good report (Philippians 4:8). Love covers a multitude of sins (1 Peter 4:8). Love edifies, speaking words that build up another person. Jesus said he didn't come to condemn, but we are condemned when we don't believe. Believe what? Believe that He is good, He loves us, He has a purpose and works all things together for good to those that love Him and are called according to purpose. Believe on Him to supply the supernatural strength and wisdom necessary to lay down our lives and walk in obedience to the Holy Spirit.

Jesus said we will be required to give an account of every idle word we have spoken. Idle in the Greek language means unemployed; (by implication) lazy, useless:–barren, idle, slow. So therefore, we see that what Jesus means is that we will give account for every lazy, useless, and barren word we speak, words that are faithless and do not operate to bring forth fruit in His kingdom.

Will we be shocked on that day as we find out what we actually were responsible for in this life? Some who have near-death experiences say they saw a movie of their life played out. As it plays, does the Spirit of Truth speak to us and tell us how differently things could have been had we believed in God's goodness and spoke forth life, giving words in situations that He placed us in? At the very least, could we have prayed?

> My brethren, be not many masters, knowing that we shall receive the greater condemnation. For in many things we offend all. If any man offend not in word, the same is a perfect man, and able also to bridle the whole body. Behold, we put bits in the horses' mouths, that they may obey us; and we turn about their whole body. Behold also the ships, which though they be so great, and are driven of fierce winds, yet are they turned about with a very small helm, whithersoever the governor listeth. Even so the tongue is a little member, and boasteth great things. Behold, how great a matter a little fire kindleth! And the tongue is a fire, a world of iniquity: so is the tongue among our members, that it defileth the whole body, and setteth on fire the

course of nature; and it is set on fire of hell. For every kind of beasts, and of birds, and of serpents, and of things in the sea, is tamed, and hath been tamed of mankind: But the tongue can no man tame; it is an unruly evil, full of deadly poison. Therewith bless we God, even the Father; and therewith curse we men, which are made after the similitude of God. Out of the same mouth proceedeth blessing and cursing. My brethren, these things ought not so to be.

James 3:1–10 (KJV)

Our words create. His words do not return void—they accomplish His purposes. In the same manner, He has given us creative power in our words—are we speaking blessing or cursing? Are the words of our mouth bitter or sweet? What are we creating? Our words will remain forever in the atmosphere—are they full of faith in Him and bringing glory to His Name, or are we creating havoc, chaos, and death?

Death and life are in the power of the tongue: and they that love it shall eat the fruit thereof.

Proverbs 18:21 (KJV)

If any man among you seem to be religious, and bridleth not his tongue, but deceiveth his own heart, this man's religion is vain.

James 1:26 (KJV)

Bridle means to curb, to be a bit-leader. To allow our tongue to speak whatever is on our mind, especially if we are in the flesh and not the spirit, will cause our own heart to be deceived. We will think we are right in our own eyes, but God will be far from us. If we don't have the presence of mind to speak His words, we should quiet ourselves until we do. Otherwise, we will eat the fruit of our words—confusion, strife, envy, wrath, etc.

But what saith it? The word is nigh thee, even in thy mouth, and in thy heart: that is, the word of faith, which we preach;

Romans 10:8 (KJV)

They would none of my counsel: they despised all my reproof. Therefore shall they eat of the fruit of their own way, and be filled with their own devices.

Proverbs 1:30–31 (KJV)

Hear, O earth: behold, I will bring evil upon this people, even the fruit of their thoughts, because they have not hearkened unto my words, nor to my law, but rejected it.

Jeremiah 6:19 (KJV)

Suffer not thy mouth to cause thy flesh to sin; neither say thou before the angel, that it was an error: wherefore should God be angry at thy voice, and destroy the work of thine hands? For in the multitude of dreams and many words there are also divers vanities: but fear thou God.

Ecclesiastes 5:6–7 (KJV)

The preparations of the heart belong to man: but the answer of the tongue is from the LORD.

Proverbs 16:1 (ERV)

I create the fruit of the lips.

Isaiah 57:19 (KJV)

The responsibility of speaking is up to us. God will give us the fruit from what we have chosen to speak. He will use our bad fruit to show us where we are; hopefully we have eyes to see what He is showing us and a heart willing to be corrected.

The captive exile hasteneth that he may be loosed, and that he should not die in the pit, nor that his bread should fail. But I am the LORD thy God, that divided the sea, whose waves roared: The LORD of hosts is his name. And I have put my words in thy mouth, and I have covered thee in the shadow of mine hand, that I may plant the heavens, and lay the foundations of the earth, and say unto Zion, Thou art my people.

Isaiah 51:14–16 (KJV)

Think of it! God wants to use our words to plant the heavens and lay the foundations of the earth! My Lord and My God, if we believed this, and committed to speak life, what a changed world we would have! His Kingdom come, His will be done, on this earth! Let's follow the exhortation of Paul as written in Hebrews 13:15 (KJV), "By him therefore let us offer the sacrifice of praise to God continually, that is, the fruit of our lips giving thanks to his name."

# SHOCKING: THE REALITY THAT GOD TESTS OUR FAITH

## *Shocking: Our Response to Our Tests May Result in Another Taking Our Place*

God is calling us to a deeper place, a place of abiding and moving forward into His kingdom, but we want to stay in the place of comfort and ease, even if we are in bondage to lesser gods. It is familiar, and we think we are in control. Our flesh wants comfort and complacency.

> And when the people complained, it displeased the LORD: and the LORD heard it; and his anger was kindled; and the fire of the LORD burnt among them, and consumed them that were in the uttermost parts of the camp. And the people cried unto Moses; and when Moses prayed unto the LORD, the fire was quenched. And he called the name of the place Taberah: because the fire of the LORD burnt among them.
>
> Numbers 11:1–3 (KJV)

The fire of God burns away all that is not holy. If you aren't in the center of the camp (the center of God's will), you will be consumed when the fire comes. We are God's covenant people, set apart for Him, to give glory to His Name. He has made many grand and glorious promises to us. When we complain, we are unbelieving, doubting His goodness and faithfulness. Our accusations bring judgment as we perceive Him incorrectly.

> And the mixed multitude in their midst lusted with great lust. And the sons of Israel also turned and wept, and said, Who shall give us flesh to eat? We remember the fish which we ate freely in Egypt, the cucumbers, and the melons, and the leeks, and the onions, and the garlic.
>
> Numbers 11:4–5 (KJV)

If we aren't in the center of the camp, surrounded by His people, we will be led away by those with a foot in the world, on the edges, not wanting to be close, drawn only so far, not truly committed. If we don't commit fully, our heart will lead us out. Our heart was created to be passionate and devoted. If we aren't devoted to spiritual things, we will be devoted to the flesh and soul. His discipline may seem harsh, but it is necessary to rid ourselves of our desire to live in the flesh.

The correct reaction to contrary or adverse circumstances is seen in Romans 4:3, 20–21. Abraham believed God, and it was accounted to him as righteousness. He did not stagger at the promise of God through unbelief but was strong in his faith and giving God glory, being fully persuaded that He was able to do that which He had promised.

God told the Israelites that He was taking them into a land of promise. He had delivered them from bondage. When the test got hard, they gave up mentally and longed for the fleshly comforts they had in Egypt, complaining about His providence. He worked with them over and over again, but from that original group only Joshua and Caleb were able to enter the Promised Land. They believed God, and because of their mindset that God was good and able to perform, they were able to have faith even when the circumstances looked contrary. The wrong perception of the same circumstances was that there were giants that they could not overcome; they viewed themselves as grasshoppers in comparison. Joshua and Caleb recognized that God was bigger than their enemies and that because He was with them, they would be able to overtake them. The others' shock was that they had to exercise control over their thoughts and will, not allowing their thoughts to be controlled by their feelings of fear, but by what God said.

God will always be merciful and pardon, when you repent, but you may not receive the promises. Putting God to the test, for example, "If you love me, you will…" shows immaturity, as we do not really know Him and His ways; we don't have the experience with Him to know He is good—all the time—and that His Word is true and He is true to His Word. We do not get to enter into the promises if we put God to the test. We are to walk by faith— trusting, believing, and obeying. When you test others, you don't really believe them and want them to prove their love. Think of a rebellious teenager, you will love and pardon them, time after time, but not until they are mature do they receive the full measure of all that you long to give them. You won't give them the keys to your car unless you trust them to follow the laws of the land and your own directives. So it is with God. He isn't going to let us walk in the fullness until we are obediently trusting and obeying; otherwise, His power in us could be the thing that destroys us and many lives around us. We would be using it for our own selfish desires. Think of the many "great" spiritual leaders that were destroyed by their own lusts. I am certain that there were occasions where they stubbornly refused to follow godly counsel and the leadership of the Holy Spirit, and their ministries were destroyed, and many sheep fell away.

> But truly, as I live, all the earth shall be filled with the glory of Jehovah. Because all those men who have seen My glory and My miracles which I did in Egypt and in the wilderness, and have tempted Me now these ten times, and have not listened to My voice, surely they shall not see the land which I swore to their fathers, neither shall any of them that provoked Me see it. But My servant Caleb, because he had another spirit with him, and has followed Me fully, I will bring him into the land into which he went. And his seed shall possess it.
>
> Numbers 14:21–24 (NKJV)

They tempted God ten times. Ten is the number of law, order, government, testing, trial, and responsibility. Testing ten times shows that they were intent on governing themselves, and this became the end of the line for them. God gave them ten opportunities to turn to Him fully and believe, and then His divine law came into play.

> And Joshua, the son of Nun, and Caleb, the son of Jephunneh, of those that searched the land, tore their clothes. And they spoke to all the company of the sons of Israel saying, The land which we passed through to search is an exceedingly good land. If Jehovah delights in us, then He will bring us into this land and give it to us, a land which flows with milk and honey. Only do not rebel against Jehovah, neither fear the people of the land. For they are bread for us. Their protection has moved from them, and Jehovah is with us. Do not fear them. But all the congregation said to stone them with stones. And the glory of Jehovah appeared in the tabernacle of the congregation before all the sons of Israel.
>
> Numbers 14:6–10 (NKJV)

The people were so set and intent in their unbelief that they wanted to kill those who gave a good report and exhorted them to believe God and enter in. Isn't this how we are when we are in the flesh? We don't want to hear anyone telling us the Word of God, talking about the things of God, etc. God would have killed them but for Moses's intercession; instead, He pardoned them; nevertheless, they could not enter into the Promised Land.

> And the LORD said unto Moses, How long will this people provoke me? and how long will it be ere they believe me, for all the signs which I have shewed among them? I will smite them with the pestilence, and disinherit them, and will make of thee a greater nation and mightier than they. And Moses said unto the LORD, Then the Egyptians shall hear it, (for thou broughtest up this people in thy might from among them;) And they will tell it to the inhabitants of this land: for they have heard that thou LORD art among this people, that thou LORD art seen face to face, and that thy cloud standeth over them, and that thou goest

before them, by day time in a pillar of a cloud, and in a pillar of fire by night. Now if thou shalt kill all this people as one man, then the nations which have heard the fame of thee will speak, saying, Because the LORD was not able to bring this people into the land which he sware unto them, therefore he hath slain them in the wilderness. And now, I beseech thee, let the power of my LORD be great, according as thou hast spoken, saying, The LORD is long-suffering, and of great mercy, forgiving iniquity and transgression, and by no means clearing the guilty, visiting the iniquity of the fathers upon the children unto the third and fourth generation. Pardon, I beseech thee, the iniquity of this people according unto the greatness of thy mercy, and as thou hast forgiven this people, from Egypt even until now. And the LORD said, I have pardoned according to thy word: But as truly as I live, all the earth shall be filled with the glory of the LORD. Because all those men which have seen my glory, and my miracles, which I did in Egypt and in the wilderness, and have tempted me now these ten times, and have not hearkened to my voice; Surely they shall not see the land which I sware unto their fathers, neither shall any of them that provoked me see it: But my servant Caleb, because he had another spirit with him, and hath followed me fully, him will I bring into the land whereinto he went; and his seed shall possess it.

Numbers 14:11–24 (KJV)

Thank God that Jesus is interceding for us. The thought that there will be an end of our trials on this earth, when God's righteous judgment will prevail, should exhort us to rightly consider Him and His ways, and spur us on to take hold of His promises and stand in faith on them, believing He is good and His grace will be sufficient for us as we take our tests. I for one do not want to get to heaven and not receive all that is stored up for me. I also don't want to find out that there were many great and precious promises that I did not receive in this life, or that others failed to receive salvation, deliverance, healing or any type of spiritual reward because of my failures. I have my regrets for those times I did not press in and found myself years behind where I should have been. God in His grace and mercy taught me from those mistakes in the schoolhouse of life, and His lessons have come back to my mind in subsequent tests. We should always be going up to the next level, and not remaining in kindergarten. Thank God for His patience! He will always be working with us and uses every experience we have, good or bad, to work toward His purposes for our life (Rom. 8:28–29).

## Shocking: God Wants to Give Us His Sight Where We Have Blind Spots

In our trials and temptations, God wants to bring us to the next level of authority, but we must listen closely to discern His instructions as it is a new area; we cannot access new territory with yesterday's anointing.

In Exodus 17, we read that Moses led the people into the wilderness, and when they came to Rephidim, there was no water. They were grumbling to Moses, accusing him of bringing them out from Egypt to die in the wilderness. Moses went to God and asked Him what to do, as the people were so angry, they wanted to stone him. God told him to take the rod he used to strike the Nile in Egypt and to bring with him elders to the rock at Horeb, to strike the rock and water would come out for the people.

> And all the congregation of the children of Israel journeyed from the wilderness of Sin, after their journeys, according to the commandment of the Lord, and pitched in Rephidim: and there was no water for the people to drink. Wherefore the people did chide with Moses, and said, Give us water that we may drink. And Moses said unto them, Why chide ye with me? wherefore do ye tempt the Lord? And the people thirsted there for water; and the people murmured against Moses, and said, Wherefore is

this that thou hast brought us up out of Egypt, to kill us and our children and our cattle with thirst? And Moses cried unto the Lord, saying, What shall I do unto this people? they be almost ready to stone me. And the Lord said unto Moses, Go on before the people, and take with thee of the elders of Israel; and thy rod, wherewith thou smotest the river, take in thine hand, and go. Behold, I will stand before thee there upon the rock in Horeb; and thou shalt smite the rock, and there shall come water out of it, that the people may drink. And Moses did so in the sight of the elders of Israel. And he called the name of the place Massah, and Meribah, because of the chiding of the children of Israel, and because they tempted the Lord, saying, Is the Lord among us, or not?

Exodus 17:1–7 (KJV)

In the next occurrence where there is no water (Num. 20), the same thing occurs where the people are complaining and Moses goes to God. This time, God tells Moses to speak to the rock. Instead, in anger, he strikes the rock twice.

Then came the children of Israel, even the whole congregation, into the desert of Zin in the first month: and the people abode in Kadesh; and Miriam died there, and was buried there. And there was no water for the congregation: and they gathered themselves together against Moses and against Aaron. And the people chode with Moses, and spake, saying, Would God that we had died when our brethren died before the LORD! And why have ye brought up the congregation of the LORD into this wilderness, that we and our cattle should die there? And wherefore have ye made us to come up out of Egypt, to bring us in unto this evil place? it is no place of seed, or of figs, or of vines, or of pomegranates; neither is there any water to drink. And Moses and Aaron went from the presence of the assembly unto the door of the tabernacle of the congregation, and they fell upon their faces: and the glory of the Lord appeared unto them. And the Lord spake unto Moses, saying, Take the rod, and gather thou the assembly together, thou, and Aaron thy brother, and speak ye unto the rock before their eyes; and it shall give forth his water, and thou shalt bring forth to them water out of the rock: so thou shalt give the congregation and their beasts drink. And Moses took the rod from before the Lord, as he commanded him. And Moses and Aaron gathered the congregation together before the rock, and he said unto them, Hear now, ye rebels; must we fetch you water out of this rock? And Moses lifted up his hand, and with his rod he smote the rock twice: and the water came out abundantly, and the congregation drank, and their beasts also. And the Lord spake unto Moses and Aaron, Because ye believed me not, to sanctify me in the eyes of the children of Israel, therefore ye shall not bring this congregation into the land which I have given them.

Numbers 20:1–12 (KJV)

The first instance of striking the rock represents Christ being smitten on our behalf. The second time, God was ready to take Moses to a new level of authority—to speak to the rock rather than smite it. The work of Christ on the cross is complete; we are now restored to the relationship with God that was intended, one of dominion as His representative and steward on this earth. The earth that was under the sway of the evil one now is to be under our sway, to the extent of the authority that God gives us in Christ. Moses succumbed to the pressure of the people clamoring, which kept him from hearing God and obeying God. He was hearing the other voices around him rather than staying focused on what God was saying. Negative voices, when internalized, produce fear and doubt rather than faith. If we don't correct the lie, we are agreeing with it; at the very least, we are allowing its place.

Moses already had a blind spot where he didn't think he could speak. Now God is telling him to speak to the rock rather than smite it. He either didn't believe it would work, because of his blind spot, or he was reacting in anger, in the flesh, to the people and may not have been fully listening. It was probably a combination of the two.

Smiting the rock with the rod gives an additional "works" facilitation that is pleasing to our flesh—a tangible, material object—something to "do" manifesting as power in the rod, rather than believing that our speaking forth the Word will produce results. There is also an inherent danger in giving power to objects—it is called idolatry.

This place was named the waters of Massah and Meribah: Massah means temptation; Meribah means strive in the wilderness of Zin (meaning thorns). Our temptation to doubt comes when we are in a place of trial, a difficult and narrow place where our flesh is pricked with thorns (desire, agitation, doubt and fear being a few examples) as Satan thrusts his fiery darts into our minds.

Temptation to doubt God comes into our lives when God, in our trials, is trying to bring us to a new level of faith. It is a trial of our faith—faith that what He said is true. Circumstances arise to tempt us to doubt; God uses the same circumstances to try our faith. We can choose to trust and believe that He is good, and be obedient to His voice, or we can react in doubt, which then creates bitter water of strife, striving against the Holy Spirit; rebelling because of the thorns in our flesh, our weaknesses, and blind spots. The enemy will always use contrary circumstances to blindside us; he knows our weaknesses and wants us to doubt God's goodness (same old story—God doesn't want you to have it, Eve). Our best strategy is to react differently; believe God! Remember that the clouds of confusion are just the dust of God's feet as He is paving the way for us into new territory.

> The Lord is slow to anger, and great in power, and will not at all acquit the wicked: the Lord hath his way in the whirlwind and in the storm, and the clouds are the dust of his feet.
>
> Nahum 1:3 (KJV)

Though it is unfamiliar and confusing, trust God! He is moving among you, bringing His purposes to pass!

God uses tests to bring us to the best. He knows our potential, what He created us for. He loves us too much to leave us groveling with the chickens when He created us to soar with the eagles! He wants to wake us up to the reality that we are in a war and that there is a kingdom available to us, but we have to fight the dragons that have kept mankind bound for too long. When we are awakened to the truth, He wants us to fight for our families, our neighborhoods, cities, state, nation, and the world; to restore His kingdom to His purposes.

## Shocking: If We Aren't Seeing His Glory, We Are Becoming Gory

> And the mixt multitude that was among them fell a lusting: and the children of Israel also wept again, and said, Who shall give us flesh to eat? We remember the fish, which we did eat in Egypt freely; the cucumbers, and the melons, and the leeks, and the onions, and the garlic: But now our soul is dried away: there is nothing at all, beside this manna, before our eyes.
>
> Numbers 11:4–6 (KJV)

What is it to fall to lusting? They yielded to intense cravings. They were sick of seeing the manna and quail, and were so dissatisfied with it they felt their whole being was dried up. After two years of manna, they no longer saw it as a blessing, as the glory of God, but loathed it. Heavy sounding, but isn't it true. We pray for a new job and then two years later are complaining. We pray for a spouse, then the feelings wear off, and we see the natural—good and bad—and aren't satisfied.

The fifteenth day of the second month after their exodus from Egypt, they had cried out to God for food, and He answered their cries.

And the whole congregation of the children of Israel murmured against Moses and Aaron in the wilderness: And the children of Israel said unto them, Would to God we had died by the hand of the Lord in the land of Egypt, when we sat by the flesh pots, and when we did eat bread to the full; for ye have brought us forth into this wilderness, to kill this whole assembly with hunger. Then said the Lord unto Moses, Behold, I will rain bread from heaven for you; and the people shall go out and gather a certain rate every day, that I may prove them, whether they will walk in my law, or no. And it shall come to pass, that on the sixth day they shall prepare that which they bring in; and it shall be twice as much as they gather daily. And Moses and Aaron said unto all the children of Israel, At even, then ye shall know that the Lord hath brought you out from the land of Egypt: And in the morning, then ye shall see the glory of the Lord; for that he heareth your murmurings against the Lord: and what are we, that ye murmur against us? Moses also said, "You will know that it was the Lord when he gives you meat to eat in the evening and all the bread you want in the morning, because he has heard your grumbling against him. Who are we? You are not grumbling against us, but against the Lord." Then Moses told Aaron, "Say to the entire Israelite community, 'Come before the Lord, for he has heard your grumbling.'" While Aaron was speaking to the whole Israelite community, they looked toward the desert, and there was the glory of the Lord appearing in the cloud. And the Lord spake unto Moses, saying, I have heard the murmurings of the children of Israel: speak unto them, saying, At even ye shall eat flesh, and in the morning ye shall be filled with bread; and ye shall know that I am the Lord your God.

Exodus 16:2–12 (kjv)

God told them that the bread from heaven was how they would see the glory of the Lord and know that the Lord brought them out of Egypt. Two years later, they were questioning His existence again. They had continued to get manna every day, but they stopped seeing it as the bread from heaven, they no longer saw the glory of God in it. They had become influenced by the clamor of the world (the mixed multitude among them) saying, "You need more, you need something different, this isn't enough." They were satisfied until they stopped seeing God and their eyes were on their lustful cravings.

> And say thou unto the people, Sanctify yourselves against to morrow, and ye shall eat flesh: for ye have wept in the ears of the Lord, saying, Who shall give us flesh to eat? for it was well with us in Egypt: therefore the Lord will give you flesh, and ye shall eat. Ye shall not eat one day, nor two days, nor five days, neither ten days, nor twenty days; But even a whole month, until it come out at your nostrils, and it be loathsome unto you: because that ye have despised the Lord which is among you, and have wept before him, saying, Why came we forth out of Egypt? And Moses said, The people, among whom I am, are six hundred thousand footmen; and thou hast said, I will give them flesh, that they may eat a whole month. Shall the flocks and the herds be slain for them, to suffice them? or shall all the fish of the sea be gathered together for them, to suffice them? And the Lord said unto Moses, Is the Lord's hand waxed short? thou shalt see now whether my word shall come to pass unto thee or not.
>
> Numbers 11:18–23 (kjv)

> And there went forth a wind from the Lord, and brought quails from the sea, and let them fall by the camp, as it were a day's journey on this side, and as it were a day's journey on the other side, round about the camp, and as it were two cubits high upon the face of the earth. And the people stood up all that day, and all that night, and all the next day, and they gathered the quails: he that gathered least gathered ten homers: and they spread them all abroad

for themselves round about the camp. And while the flesh was yet between their teeth, ere it was chewed, the wrath of the LORD was kindled against the people, and the LORD smote the people with a very great plague. And he called the name of that place Kibrothhattaavah: because there they buried the people that lusted. And the people journeyed from Kibrothhattaavah unto Hazeroth; and abode at Hazeroth.

Numbers 11:31–35 (KJV)

Plague in the Hebrew language means a blow, a wound, pestilence. They said their soul dried away because they only "saw" manna before their eyes. True, if we only see manna, as the grain, before our eyes, and don't recognize the glory of God, our soul will dry up, and our heart will become hard to God's goodness.

What was the plague? They received graves of lusting because they were not thankful and forgot that their provision was the glory of God shown to them. Those that lusted received the plague and died.

In Romans we read that we see the glory of God in creation itself. When we aren't thankful and don't glorify God in our hearts, He gives us over to uncleanness in the lusts of our hearts, and our thoughts became futile and our hearts hardened (Rom. 1:21–24). We may not die physically, but when God gives us over to our lusts, we die spiritually, and our soul becomes dry and empty; the promises of God die; our kingdom inheritance is now dead to us. Thanks be to God for His mercy; as long as we are in this body during our sojourn on the earth, we can repent and turn back to Him and to His purposes.

We are called to a high place, created in His image, to speak forth the truth and see His kingdom manifested here on earth. Everything exists first in the spirit, conceived by God, then spoken into existence. He is trying to get us into a higher place, seeing what already exists in heaven, hearing the thing that He desires to bring to the earth, then believe Him, speak it forth, and wait patiently for His kingdom to manifest on the earth. Waiting patiently means continuing to believe that it already exists in Him; walk and speak as if it does!

> Behold, the former things are come to pass, and new things do I declare: before they spring forth I tell you of them.
>
> Isaiah 42:9 (KJV)

> And who, as I, shall call, and shall declare it, and set it in order for me, since I appointed the ancient people? and the things that are coming, and shall come, let them shew unto them. Fear ye not, neither be afraid: have not I told thee from that time, and have declared it? ye are even my witnesses. Is there a God beside me? yea, there is no God; I know not any.
>
> Isaiah 44:7–8 (KJV)

> (As it is written, I have made thee a father of many nations,) before him whom he believed, even God, who quickeneth the dead, and calleth those things which be not as though they were.
>
> Romans 4:17 (KJV)

> Surely the Lord GOD will do nothing, but he revealeth his secret unto his servants the prophets. The lion hath roared, who will not fear? the Lord GOD hath spoken, who can but prophesy? Publish in the palaces at Ashdod, and in the palaces in the land of Egypt, and say, Assemble yourselves upon the mountains of Samaria, and behold the great tumults in the midst thereof, and the oppressed in the midst thereof.
>
> Amos 3:7–9 (KJV)

We are all called to prophesy—to speak forth what God has spoken to us, to continue to stand steadfast upon His word until we see it come to pass, and even after, to not let the enemy come back in we must maintain our ground. We are His vessels here on the earth. We are to declare His kingdom. Thy kingdom come, Thy will be done, on earth as it is in heaven. This is what we are believing for—His kingdom to be restored and established!

The Word became flesh; God spoke, and it was so. When God speaks to us, we are to speak it forth into the atmosphere. We are His mouthpieces, vessels set apart for His use. He is looking for one whose heart is perfect toward Him (2 Chronicles 16:9), a heart perfectly positioned in a posture toward Him. Our being should be ever poised toward Him—body, soul, and spirit. With our body, we speak His words so that His kingdom will be made manifest on earth as it is in heaven.

What of those occasions when Jesus did not speak, or answered in a way that didn't seem to answer the question? Jesus only spoke what He heard the Father speak. So are we to do. The Father knows what needs to be said and done in order for His Kingdom to come. As we listen in accuracy and submit to His authority, the bride will be spotless and Jesus will be made known. Let the Spirit and the bride say, "Come, Lord Jesus."

Half of the battle is showing up, that is, putting ourselves in the position to hear, not allowing ourselves to be distracted. That is one of the enemy's tactics in this age, to keep us so busy that we are too frantic and worn out to pay attention to the still, small voice of the Holy Spirit.

> And he shall speak great words against the most High, and shall wear out the saints of the most High, and think to change times and laws: and they shall be given into his hand until a time and times and the dividing of time.
>
> Daniel 7:25 (KJV)

"Wear out" in Strong's Concordance means to afflict mentally, and the root of it means to fail; by implication to wear out, decay, cause to consume, spend and waste.[15]

Isn't it true that we are often so busy wasting our time and energy consuming, and it causes us to be worn out, our health and mental state failing because it is taxed with so many projects, things to do and things to buy? I can remember when I was growing up, my mom went food shopping once every two weeks (we had milk delivered in those days). And there certainly was not the onslaught on the television commercials blasting us with images of what we "need." Remember, the eye is never satisfied (Prov. 27:20), and the lust of the eyes and flesh are not of the Father, but of the world (1 John 2:16). Jesus strongly rebuked the man who thought he could store up goods to consume them later (Luke 12:16–21). Consumerism (covetousness) will kill our spirit life, keeping us out of position to receive from God (Luke 12:15; 1 Cor. 6:9–10; Eph. 5:5). Perhaps when we aren't seeing or hearing God, we should ask ourselves if we have set up an idol in our hearts, spending our time seeking things that the world offers rather than His kingdom.

## *Shocking: Unbelief Blinds Us from Seeing Reality*

In Genesis 16:10-11, 21:14, and Galatians 4:24, we read of Hagar. What a story. We have heard many times of the promise God gave to Abraham and Sarah of a son, how they took matters into their own hands and brought forth an Ishmael; we have heard of the miracle that in the time of life when Sarah's womb was dried up that she conceived; we have heard of the faith of Abraham as he went forth with Isaac to sacrifice and how God brought forth a lamb.

Yet there is a shockingly beautiful account of faith with Hagar, Sarah's servant. Given over to Abraham to bear his son because Sarah and Abraham took matters into their own hands, she was then viewed with jealousy after the son (Ishmael) was born. When Sarah dealt harshly with her, she ran into the wilderness (desert). An angel sent by the Lord found her by a fountain of water.

And the angel of the LORD said unto her, Return to thy mistress, and submit thyself under her hands. And the angel of the LORD said unto her, I will multiply thy seed exceedingly, that it shall not be numbered for multitude. And the angel of the LORD said unto her, Behold, thou are with child, and shall bear a son, and shall call his name Ishmael (God shall hear); because the LORD hath heard thy affliction…And she called the name of the LORD that spake unto her, Thou God seest me: for she said, Have I also seen after Him that seeth me? Wherefore the well was called Beer-lahoi-roi;…(the well of Him that liveth and seeth me.)

Genesis 16:9–14 (KJV)

God revealed Himself to Hagar as the God who lives and who sees her. Now fast-forward to Genesis, chapter 21, fifteen years later. This time Hagar and Ishmael were sent out by Abraham and Sarah.

And she departed, and wandered in the wilderness of Beer-sheba (well of the oath). Abraham had given her bread and water. The water was gone, so she cast Ishmael under a shrub, and she went and sat down over against a good way off…so as not to see his death. Then she lifted up her voice and wept.

Genesis 21:14 (KJV)

And God heard the voice of the lad and the angel of God called to Hagar out of heaven and said unto her, What aileth thee, Hagar? Fear not: for God hath heard the voice of the lad where he is.

Genesis 21:17 (KJV)

And God opened her eyes, and she saw a well of water.

Genesis 21:19 (KJV)

The well didn't just appear; it was already there! She had for-gotten the word God had given her about Ishmael, forgotten that she named a well, "the well of Him that liveth and seeth me." She was blinded by her circumstances. She could only see despair, hopelessness and death, although the well was there all along. Prophetically, Ishmael means, "God shall hear." I'm certain that Hagar told Ishmael of her earlier experience, of his birth and the prophecies. In verse 17 we read that it was Ishmael that cried out and whom God heard. An angel told Hagar that God had heard the voice of the lad then God opened Hagar's eyes to see the well.

Hagar was shocked in her desert experience. Too often when we are in our desert, we forget that the promises of God are "yea" and "amen." God always keeps His word. It is as if a veil is over our eyes; in fact, a veil is over our eyes. We have forgotten that the veil was torn in two when Jesus died after taking our sins upon himself and we now have free access to the Father, to the kingdom, if we have faith. We are blinded by our circumstances. Open our eyes, Lord, to the fullness of the gospel.

> And not as Moses, which put a vail over his face, that the children of Israel could not steadfastly look to the end of that which is abolished: But their minds were blinded: for until this day remaineth the same vail untaken away in the reading of the old testament; which vail is done away in Christ. But even unto this day, when Moses is read, the vail is upon their heart. Nevertheless when it shall turn to the Lord, the vail shall be taken away. Now the Lord is that Spirit: and where the Spirit of the Lord is, there is lib-erty. But we all, with open face beholding as in a glass the glory of the Lord, are changed into the same image from glory to glory, even as by the Spirit of the Lord.
>
> 2 Corinthians 3:13–18 (KJV)

> But also if our gospel is hidden, it is hidden to those being lost, in whom the god of this world has blinded the minds

of the unbelieving ones, so that the light of the glorious gospel of Christ (who is the image of God) should not dawn on them. For we do not preach ourselves, but Christ Jesus as Lord, and ourselves your servants for Jesus's sake. For it is God who said, "Out of darkness Light shall shine;" who shone in our hearts to give the brightness of the knowledge of the glory of God in the face of Jesus Christ.

2 Corinthians 4:3–6 (NKJV)

Yet the beauty of God's grace is that He uses the blinding circumstances to bring forth His Word as true, alive, and glorious. He is our patient teacher, showing us His faithfulness to His Word and our weakness in our flesh, to teach us to live by faith in every word that proceeds from the mouth of God (Deut. 8:3; Matt. 4:4).

## *Shocking: God "Refines" Our Faith in Adversity*

In 1 Kings 17, we read that after Elijah spoke the Word of the Lord to Ahab that there would be a three-year drought, God sent Elijah to the brook Cherith near Jordan. God told Elijah that the ravens would feed him there and that he would drink of the brook. After the brook dried up, God told Elijah to go to Zarephath, which means place of refinement. He told Elijah that He had commanded a widow woman at Zarephath to make provision for him. Elijah went; as he entered the city, he saw the widow gathering sticks and asked her to fetch him some water to drink. As she went (confirming to him that this was the woman), he asked her to also bring him some bread.

And she said, As the LORD thy God liveth, I have not a cake, but an handful of meal in a barrel, and a little oil in a cruse: and, behold, I am gathering two sticks, that I may go in and dress it for me and my son, that we may eat it, and die. And Elijah said unto her, Fear not; go and do as thou hast said: but make me thereof a little cake first, and bring it unto me, and after make for thee and for thy son. For thus saith the LORD God of Israel, The barrel of meal shall not waste, neither shall the cruse of oil fail, until the day that the LORD sendeth rain upon the earth. And she went and did according to the saying of Elijah: and she, and he, and her house, did eat many days. And the barrel of meal wasted not, neither did the cruse of oil fail, according to the word of the LORD, which he spake by Elijah.

1Kings 17:12–16 (KJV)

God had spoken to this woman that He was sending a messenger to her. She said to Elijah that all she had was a handful of meal and a little oil. Elijah asked her to make him a cake first, then one for her and her son, and that the Lord God says that the meal and the oil would not be depleted until He sends rain again. She believed and received. This alone is miraculous and faith building. Yet God didn't stop there. Remember, this is a place of refinement. She will soon have her faith built upon the rock of everlasting life, the resurrection power of God. Elijah's faith will also be refined.

And it came to pass after these things, that the son of the woman, the mistress of the house, fell sick; and his sickness was so sore, that there was no breath left in him. And she said unto Elijah, What have I to do with thee, O thou man of God? art thou come unto me to call my sin to remembrance, and to slay my son? And he said unto her, Give me thy son. And he took him out of her bosom, and carried him up into a loft, where he abode, and laid him upon his own bed. And he cried unto the LORD, and said, O LORD my God, hast thou also brought evil upon the widow with whom I sojourn, by slaying her son? And he stretched himself upon the child three times, and cried unto the LORD, and said, O LORD my God, I pray thee, let this child's soul come into him again. And the LORD heard the voice of Elijah; and the soul of the child came into him again, and he revived. And Elijah took the child, and brought him down out of the chamber into the house, and delivered him unto his mother: and Elijah said, See, thy son liveth. And the woman said to Elijah, Now by this I know that thou art a man of God, and that the word of the LORD in thy mouth is truth.

1Kings 17:12–16 (KJV)

When her son became ill and died, the woman immediately thought it was because of her sin. We don't know what her sin was, and I believe that it is omitted on purpose so that we can all identify. When bad things happen, don't we automatically think it is because we did something wrong, that we are being punished? No, in this harsh circumstance her faith was to be refined. She did not stop at the place of fear, guilt, and shame. She took hold of the word that the Lord gave her, that the meal and oil would sustain them until rain came again. Sustain does not mean die. She also knew that she had been faithfully providing for the representative of God. She brought her son to Elijah who stretched himself over the child three times: the Israelites were three days in the wilderness with no water; three days crossing the Jordan into the promised land; David was revived after three days; after three days Jesus rose from the grave; Saul/Paul was blind three days before his vision was restored. The number three is significant, representing life over death.

Elijah's faith also was refined; he also first thought (or came into agreement with her fear) that God was bringing evil to slay her son. Yet there was a seed of faith in Elijah; he had to stretch his faith over the circumstances in the natural, over the lies of the devil, and stand on the knowledge that God is good, not evil. God would not be glorified in the death of the child. Elijah took the boy out of her bosom (bosom representing the flesh/soul) and carried him to the loft, the place where he abode (loft representing the higher place of the spirit). He placed the boy on his bed, the place of rest. When we rest upon the finished work of Christ, our faith produces the fertile ground for God to perform the miracles we need. Yet for a moment he, being human, was influenced by her thoughts of evil and asked God if that is what happened (bringing her sin to remembrance). Yet he knew God's goodness and stepped out in faith, believing! This is the place of refinement of our faith—continuing to believe in God's promises and His goodness when circumstances seem to state otherwise, and the enemy and our own flesh make war against our faith.

Our faith will be tested over and over again as God brings us into situations He has orchestrated for our growth into the destiny in Christ that He has for us. In the moment where our circumstances are most contrary to His promises is exactly where we need to stand firm and stretch our faith over our situation. Elijah "stretched" himself over the boy. The word stretched means to stretch oneself, to measure, to be extended. He had to look at his faith in light of the circumstance and stretch, or extend, his faith to a greater measure. At that moment, he then cried to the Lord praying that God would let the child's soul come into him again.

God heard the voice of Elijah, and the soul of the child came into him again, and he revived. In this scripture reference, Strong's Concordance indicates that the word heard means to hear intelligently, with implication of attention and obedience; to consider and consent; to perceive and proclaim; to show forth.[16] God did not respond to the unbelief, the faithless words.

It was not until Elijah stretched himself that God heard faith. God responds to faith. When we speak words of life, full of faith in God's ability, He responds. Let God have His way in our Zarephath seasons so that He can do mighty works in this generation and be glorified.

In Luke 4:26, Jesus notes that in this three-and-a-half-year period of drought, there were many widows, but Elijah was only sent to one. The context is that a prophet is not accepted in his own country; though God desires to do a work, most people do not believe. I wonder how many Christians have had the Holy Spirit speak a word of life and their mind immediately argues against it with its reasons. God tells us to reason with Him, knowing that when we bring our reasoning to Him, the Holy Spirit will respond with the Truth, and we will recognize that He is so much bigger. If we keep our reasoning inside, it replays over and over in our minds.

The Bible is full of the words of the Lord, prophecy revealed and fulfilled in Jesus Christ. He is the healer, deliverer, redeemer, savior, provider of all. Yet do we take the time to meditate on the Word of God, or to wait upon His presence, crying out to Him day and night, until we receive in the spirit and then declare into the atmosphere so that it can be manifested in the natural in God's timing? Will we let God shock us and refine our faith so that He can bring life to dead situations in ours and others' lives, or do we want to be right in our own understanding and stay where we are in our faith walk?

## Shocking: It Will Seem We Have an Adversary When We Are Contrary to God; He Sometimes Uses Adversarial Means to Correct Us

In Numbers chapters 22-24 we read the account of Balaam. Balaam was shocked when his donkey spoke. Who wouldn't be? As a prophet, he heard from God on a regular basis. Balaam's desire to be honored by man shut his eyes from seeing spiritually. His heart wasn't right. As a prophet, he had the prophetic gift to hear from God, but his heart was in it for the reward. Only the pure in heart will see God (Matt. 5:8). Interesting that one can hear from God and even be used by God, but may not be able to "see" spiritually. If you cannot see spiritually, what you hear will be warped, perceived, seen through marred lenses, distorted by the mind of the flesh.

Although a prophet, and recognizing God's omnipotence and his own responsibility to say only what God tells him to say, he uses the situation to get what he can out of it. He knew from the beginning what God said. However, he also allowed his prophetic gift to be used for gain, since he was approached by messengers of Moab with the "diviner's fee." Balak wanted him to speak prophetically and curse Israel. Balaam was told immediately by God that he was not to curse Israel, for they are blessed, but he did not tell Balak that. He only told him God wouldn't let him go with him. Yet he was swayed by the prospect of reward (2 Pet. 2:15), asking God over and over if he could go. Each time he attempted to get God to say more on the matter. The second time, God told him, "If the men come to call you, rise and go with them; but yet the word that I shall say unto thee, that shall thou do" (Num. 22:20). He rose and went, but the scripture doesn't say the men called him, and God didn't speak. He was stopped by his donkey refusing to move, because the donkey saw the angel of the Lord standing in the way with a drawn sword, stopping them. Yet

Balaam didn't see the angel and struck the donkey three times. The angel of the Lord said to him, "Why have you struck your donkey these three times? Behold, I have come out as an adversary, because your way was contrary to me" (Num. 22:32 NASV). When we are contrary to God and His purpose, it will seem that the enemy is the adversary against us, blocking us from our path. We think the enemy means to harm us, but God is sending an adversary because our ways are contrary to His. He is trying to get us back on track.

If the donkey had not turned, the angel said he would have slain Balaam (Num. 22:33). This is hard to think about, that God may allow some to die so that they do not continue on a path that will destroy others and/or avert God's purpose. Ironically, Balaam told the donkey if he'd had a sword he would have killed it. The angel said if the donkey hadn't turned, he would have killed Balaam.

Balaak took Balaam to the high places (representing idol worship) three times (Num. 23 and 24). The second time, Balaam went looking for "enchantments." Strong's Concordance tells us that the word enchantments means to hiss, to whisper, magic spell, to prognosticate.[17] Prognosticate, according to Webster's Dictionary, is predicting/fortune-telling, using present indications as a guide. [18]

The danger and warning is to rely on things we see in the natural and use natural things to predict the future in the way we want it to look. Trying to manipulate and control our circumstances and others is witchcraft. God's ways are higher than ours. He creates the natural, and at His word, it moves.

The first two times, Balaam had performed a ritual to try and sway God and/or to impress man, indicated by the altars, or "going to meet God." He already knew what God had to say about it; God had already told him. In Numbers 23:23, God told Balaam that there is no enchantment or divination that will work against Israel. In Numbers 24:1, it says that this time Balaam set his face to the "wilderness," and the Spirit of God came upon him, where he saw an open vision in addition to hearing the words. When he stopped trying to sway God and get honor from man, seeing that his trickery was of no use, his prophetic gift was opened again, and he saw an open vision. Spiritual gifts are from God. If you are trying to manipulate God for your own gain, you will not be able to flow in your gifts to the fullest extent that God intends.

Though Balaam could not curse the children of Israel, he told Balaak how to get them to be cursed—to stop walking with God; to worship idols, joining themselves to the ungodly and taking on their ways. This would bring the curse upon them (Rev: 2:14).

We read in Numbers 31:1 that the children of Israel, through Balaam, trespassed against the Lord in the matter of Peor, and there was a plague. They joined themselves to Baal-Peor, lord of the gap. In Strong's Concordance, this means, having eyes set upon waste, bringing a plague and destruction.[19]

I believe the application to our lives is that when we stop seeking God and begin to worship worldly things that produce nothing of eternal value, we cause a gap in our spiritual life, and death begins to work. When we set our eyes upon God, He brings abundance, fertility, beauty, prosperity, strength, and order.

God has given us creative power. What we set our eyes upon, we begin to desire, and the desires of our hearts bring forth the words from our mouths (Luke 6:45). We eat from the fruit of our lips (Prov. 18:20). Proverbs 27:20 tells us that the eye is never satisfied. 1 John 2:16 tells us that all that is in the world—the lust of the eyes, the lust of the flesh, and the pride of life—is not of the Father, but of the world.

God will work with us to show us where we are, trying to get us in line with His purposes, even to the extent of using adversarial means to correct us. In 1 Kings 12:24 (KJV), we see that what seemed a matter of evil against them and a cause for war was actually the hand of the Lord. "Thus saith the Lord, Ye shall not go up, nor fight against your brethren the children of

Israel: return every man to his house; for this thing is from me."
We would be wise to consider God's sovereignty when we are in
adversity and ask Him the purpose.

## *Shocking: There Will Always Be Testing of Our Faith, of What We Are Believing*

And it shall be when Jehovah your God has brought you
into the land which He swore to your fathers, to Abraham,
to Isaac, and to Jacob, to give you great and good cities
which you did not build, and houses full of every good
thing which you did not fill, and wells which are dug, but
which you did not dig, vineyards and olive trees which you
did not plant, and you shall eat and be full, you shall be on
guard lest you forget Jehovah who brought you forth out
of the land of Egypt, from the house of slaves. You shall
fear Jehovah your God and serve Him, and shall swear by
His name. You shall not go after other gods, of the gods of
the people all around you, for Jehovah your God is a jealous God among you, lest the anger of Jehovah your God
be kindled against you and destroy you from off the face
of the earth. You shall not tempt Jehovah your God as you
tempted in Massah.

Deuteronomy 6:10–16 (NKJV)

The temptation of the children of Israel was not to ask in faith
for their needs, but to disbelieve God's goodness, forgetting He
brought them out to bring them in...would a good father not
give what is needed? Ask!

It seems so simple; the difficulty in this is that it seems easier
to go after the things of the world, the way the world does it. We
don't like to wait. God often wants us to wait, to see if we will
believe and trust in His faithfulness. Also, the world wants recognition for its accomplishments; our flesh will want to exalt in
thinking that somehow it is something in us that brought God's
favor and blessing, and as soon as we start thinking that way,

we are easily deceived into thinking we created the blessing ourselves. It isn't a large leap from one to the other. The deception is combated by the reality that God wants the glory. He blesses us because He loves us, not that we are worthy of the love, but because He created us to be in His image and He is love. It is His Name that is glorified by His blessing upon us, and it is why pride will be punished. Nebuchadnezzer and Herod were both destroyed when they took upon themselves the glory due unto God (Daniel, chapter 4; Acts 12:23).

I never thought that I would be tempted in this way. In the year 2000, God blessed me with a great job that turned into a career. I had been tasked with a project that was way beyond my abilities, and I had to rely on God for wisdom, knowledge, and direction daily. Over time, this project turned into a career, where I was managing a $4,000,000-plus budget, many programs and grants, as well as a number of employees. There came a point when my identity was more in those programs and my knowledge than in being His servant. I became greedy for more (anything outside of Him doesn't satisfy and creates an insatiable demand for more). Pretty soon I was overwhelmed and stressed and no longer able to manage everything. My marriage suffered, my ministry suffered, my health suffered. When it became the point of no return, so to speak, I ended up in the hospital. Looking back, I can see that God was drawing me away from the career for a year prior. Had I listened, I could have saved myself a lot of heartache and physical suffering. However, God, in His goodness, began a restoration process, and now my marriage is better than it ever was. I am more sensitive to my body and soul so that I don't become outbalanced so easily. This restoration process brought my husband and me to a place where we are now connected to an apostolic ministry that we are certain God placed us in, for His purposes and in His timing. God works all things together for good to those who are called according to His purposes, according to Romans 8:28.

In Deuteronomy, chapter 7, the Lord tells us that we are to destroy all the false gods of the world and the graven images, as we come into the lands He gives us. We are to utterly destroy them, or they will be a snare to us. The offensive things are absorbed into us by not destroying them and will bring offense against the life of Christ in us and trap us into a lower realm, of servitude to those very things.

> Their idols are silver and gold, the work of men's hands. They have mouths, but they speak not: eyes have they, but they see not: They have ears, but they hear not: noses have they, but they smell not: They have hands, but they handle not: feet have they, but they walk not: neither speak they through their throat. They that make them are like unto them; so is every one that trusteth in them.
>
> Psalms 115:4–8 (KJV)

> Therefore, know that Jehovah your God, He is God, the faithful God who keeps covenant and mercy with them that love Him and keep His commandments, to a thousand generations. And He repays those who hate Him to their face, to destroy them. He will not be slow to repay him who hates Him. He will repay him to his face.
>
> Deuteronomy 7:9–10 (NKJV)

In this scripture, face in the Hebrew language means the part that turns—we choose which way we will turn—to God or away from Him. The creative power of God will be reflecting back to us, magnifying, so to speak, whatever we are turned toward. If we have spiritual eyes, we can see our circumstances, testing our faith, and use them to move forward into greater realms of His glory! God, open our eyes to see spiritually, that we can do mighty exploits for you and bring glory to Your name!

## Shocking: If the World Is in Your Sight, God Won't Be (Ungodly Covenants and Covetousness)

Else if ye do in any wise go back, and cleave unto the remnant of these nations, even these that remain among you, and shall make marriages with them, and go in unto them, and they to you: Know for a certainty that the LORD your God will no more drive out any of these nations from before you; but they shall be snares and traps unto you, and scourges in your sides, and thorns in your eyes, until ye perish from off this good land which the LORD your god hath given you. When ye have transgressed the covenant of the LORD your God, which he commanded you, and have gone and served other gods, and bowed yourselves to them; then shall the anger of the LORD be kindled against you, and ye shall perish quickly from off the good land which he hath given unto you.

(Joshua 23:12–13; 16)

If you join/cling to the ungodly and make bonds with them, allegiances, yokes, marriages, bowing to the other gods (compromising; submitting, lowering your standards, and not walking in uprightness of heart), then the anger (according to Strong's this means the breath or the face)[20] will be against you.

When you turn away in your heart, you are turning away from the light of His countenance; spiritually, turning your back to Him. Blessing flows from His face. If you turn from Him, you can't receive—you are now away from Him. He hasn't moved away from you; you have moved away from Him!

Now therefore put away, said he, the strange gods which are among you, and incline your heart unto the Lord God of Israel (Josh. 24:23).

To incline your heart unto God is to bend in submission to Him. God is gracious. If we but look and admit when our hearts are not inclined to Him, and ask for His help, He will help us do it!

> What prayer and supplication soever be made by any man, or by all thy people Israel, which shall know every man the plague of his own heart, and spread forth his hands toward this house: Then hear thou in heaven thy dwelling place, and forgive, and do, and give to every man according to his ways, whose heart thou knowest; (for thou, even thou only, knowest the hearts of all the children of men;)
>
> 1 Kings 8:38–39 (KJV)

> If they sin against thee, (for there is no man that sinneth not,) and thou be angry with them, and deliver them to the enemy, so that they carry them away captives unto the land of the enemy, far or near; Yet if they shall bethink themselves in the land whither they were carried captives, and repent, and make supplication unto thee in the land of them that carried them captives, saying, We have sinned, and have done perversely, we have committed wickedness; And so return unto thee with all their heart, and with all their soul, in the land of their enemies, which led them away captive, and pray unto thee toward their land, which thou gavest unto their fathers, the city which thou hast chosen, and the house which I have built for thy name: Then hear thou their prayer and their supplication in heaven thy dwelling place, and maintain their cause.
>
> 1 Kings 8:46–49 (KJV)

> If we confess our sins, he is faithful and just to forgive us our sins, and to cleanse us from all unrighteousness.
>
> 1 John 1:9 (KJV)

Why do our hearts turn away from Him? When we covet what we don't have (are not satisfied with Him and His provision), our hearts begin to turn away. If we analyze covetousness, the fact that we want something we don't have, aren't we in essence saying that God is holding back on us, He doesn't meet our needs; we want to be our own god and control our own life? Sound familiar? Seems to me to be the Garden of Eden all over again, replayed time and time again in our lives. I pray in agreement with King David, "Incline my heart unto thy testimonies and not to covetousness" (Ps. 119:36). We are clearly warned throughout scripture of the dangers of covetousness.

> And he said unto them, Take heed, and beware of covetousness: for a man's life consisteth not in the abundance of the things which he possesseth.
>
> Luke 12:15 (KJV)

> And take good heed to yourselves that you love Jehovah your God. Otherwise, if you go back in any way, and hold to those left of these nations, these that remain among you, and shall marry them and go in to them and they to you, know for a certainty that Jehovah your God will no more drive out these nations from before you. But they shall be snares and traps to you, and scourges in your sides, and thorns in your eyes, until you perish from off this good land which Jehovah your God has given you.
>
> Joshua 23:11–13 (NKJV)

According to Strong's Concordance, the word snare means to spread out a net.[21] In the dictionary, to be snared is anything that serves to entangle, trap, or catch out the unwary.[22] Traps in Strong's Concordance means a noose for catching animals, a hook for the nose, and scourges means to pierce; a flog or goad.[23] In Webster's Dictionary, we see that a goad is a long, pointed stick to prod animals; something that prods or urges; a stimulus or irritating incentive.[24] Thorns, in Strong's Concordance, refers to pricking, to clip off. [25]

So we can see that snares, traps, scourges, and thorns are things that hinder our walk and our vision. Entanglements with the world will render us unable to see or perceive God, to remember the dreams He's given us; all we will see are the hindrances. What is the world? The world is the lust of the eyes, the lust of the flesh, and the pride of life. We read in 1 John 2:16 that all that is in the world, the lust of the flesh, and the lust of the eyes, and the pride of life, is not of the Father, but is of the world.

Joshua 9, 10:4–15, and 2 Samuel 21:1–14 are lessons warning us against not seeking God's guidance and warning against making covenant with the ungodly. Covenants with the ungodly will bring division in the ranks. Joshua was deceived; he didn't seek God's counsel and went into a league with the Gibeonites. They became a snare, causing unnecessary wars and strife, because of the covenants the Gibeonites had made with others. The Israelites ended up fighting the Gibeonites' battles also. When we are yoked with the ungodly, we will end up wasting time fighting their battles.

The Lord had given clear and extensive direction about this, through Moses, when they were preparing to enter the Promised Land. How was Joshua deceived? He was deceived by wolves in sheep's clothing—they dressed themselves to look as ambassadors, and they said they had heard of the fame of the Lord God and wanted to be their servants, and make a covenant with them. They were liars—they didn't want to be destroyed, but they were not as they professed and became a snare to the Israelites. How often are we deceived by people who look good and sound good? How many times could our problems have been avoided if we had first asked God for wisdom and direction?

Time and time again we see that when we reach a place God has brought us, our tendency is to think we can now figure it out on our own. Yet there is hope—when we turn again to the Lord He causes all things to turn to our good, for His purposes to be fulfilled. What did Joshua and the elders do? They made the enemy serve them. They did not give them freedom and equal rights—

they were forced to draw water and hew wood. We can use the defeats in our lives, the places we were deceived, to become a place that brings us water and that we can build upon. The stance we take in the spirit regarding our enemies is critical. Even in areas where we have situations that seem impossible because of oaths, vows, and promises we have made, God can alter the course to be realigned to His purposes with His direction and intervention.

When you make advancements spiritually, going forward into what God has promised you, the enemy will gather forces against you and attack. In Joshua 10, we read that when Adoni-Zedek, king of Jerusalem, heard of the conquests, he feared, encamped before Gibeon to make war against them, and joined forces with four other cities to smite them when they came to Gibeon. The Lord said, "Fear them not: for I have delivered into thine hand; there shall not a man of them stand before thee."

Remember, when you start to feel sorry for these people that are being destroyed, these are nations that served the gods of sex and fertility, snakes, sacrificing their children on altars. Historical records prove this. They bring a curse upon the land—God desires to bring His kingdom to the earth, to redeem it. He loves these people too, and all creation bears witness to His greatness and power. He desires to restore them to their intended purpose, but they must choose to turn from their idols to Him, the one true God, recognizing their sin and believing in and receiving the atoning work of Jesus.

God keeps His word. The Lord routed the enemy and chased them—they were killed as he cast great hailstones from heaven, more than those killed with the sword. He said, "Fear them not: for I have delivered into thine hand; there shall not a man of them stand before thee" (Josh. 10:8). God keeps His word. We are tested every time God speaks and we hear—do we believe? The enemy will use circumstances to stonewall us, to distract us, to deceive us, trying to divert us from triumph. We are in a war. It is imperative that we keep God in our sight and His words in our heart, to be victorious.

# SHOCKING: THE REALITY OF SPIRITUAL AUTHORITY

## *Shocking: When You Presume, You Bring Doom*

### THE REBELLION OF KORAH

I am including Numbers chapter 16 in its entirety because I believe the lessons it teaches are critical to the Body of Christ in this hour.

> Now Korah, the son of Izhar, the son of Kohath, the son of Levi, and Dathan and Abiram, the sons of Eliab, and On, the son of Peleth, sons of Reuben, took men: And they rose up before Moses, with certain of the children of Israel, two hundred and fifty princes of the assembly, famous in the congregation, men of renown: And they gathered themselves together against Moses and against Aaron, and said unto them, Ye take too much upon you, seeing all the congregation are holy, every one of them, and the LORD is among them: wherefore then lift ye up yourselves above the congregation of the LORD? And when Moses heard it, he fell upon his face: And he spake unto Korah and unto all his company, saying, Even to morrow the LORD will shew who are his, and who is holy; and will cause him to come near unto him: even him whom he hath chosen will he cause to come near unto him. This do; Take you censers, Korah, and all his company; And put fire therein, and put incense in them before the LORD to morrow: and it shall be that the man whom the LORD doth choose, he shall be holy: ye take too much upon you, ye sons of Levi. And Moses said unto Korah, Hear, I pray you, ye sons of Levi: Seemeth it but a small thing unto you, that the God of Israel hath separated you from the congregation of Israel, to bring you near to himself to do the service of the tabernacle of the LORD, and

to stand before the congregation to minister unto them? And he hath brought thee near to him, and all thy brethren the sons of Levi with thee: and seek ye the priesthood also? For which cause both thou and all thy company are gathered together against the LORD: and what is Aaron, that ye murmur against him? And Moses sent to call Dathan and Abiram, the sons of Eliab: which said, We will not come up: Is it a small thing that thou hast brought us up out of a land that floweth with milk and honey, to kill us in the wilderness, except thou make thyself altogether a prince over us? Moreover thou hast not brought us into a land that floweth with milk and honey, or given us inheritance of fields and vineyards: wilt thou put out the eyes of these men? we will not come up. And Moses was very wroth, and said unto the LORD, Respect not thou their offering: I have not taken one ass from them, neither have I hurt one of them. And Moses said unto Korah, Be thou and all thy company before the LORD, thou, and they, and Aaron, to morrow: And take every man his censer, and put incense in them, and bring ye before the LORD every man his censer, two hundred and fifty censers; thou also, and Aaron, each of you his censer. And they took every man his censer, and put fire in them, and laid incense thereon, and stood in the door of the tabernacle of the congregation with Moses and Aaron. And Korah gathered all the congregation against them unto the door of the tabernacle of the congregation: and the glory of the LORD appeared unto all the congregation. And the LORD spake unto Moses and unto Aaron, saying, Separate yourselves from among this congregation, that I may consume them in a moment. And they fell upon their faces, and said, O God, the God of the spirits of all flesh, shall one man sin, and wilt thou be wroth with all the congregation? And the LORD spake unto Moses, saying, Speak unto the congregation, saying, Get you up from about the tabernacle of Korah, Dathan, and Abiram. And Moses rose up and went unto Dathan and Abiram; and the elders of Israel followed him. And he spake unto the congregation, saying, Depart, I pray you, from the tents of these wicked men, and touch nothing of theirs, lest ye be consumed in all their sins. So they gat up from the tabernacle of Korah, Dathan, and Abiram, on every side: and Dathan and Abiram came out, and stood in the door of their tents, and their wives, and their sons, and their little children. And Moses said, Hereby ye shall know that the Lord hath sent me to do all these works; for I have not done them of mine own mind. If these men die the common death of all men, or if they be visited after the visitation of all men; then the Lord hath not sent me. But if the Lord make a new thing, and the earth open her mouth, and swallow them up, with all that appertain unto them, and they go down quick into the pit; then ye shall understand that these men have provoked the Lord. And it came to pass, as he had made an end of speaking all these words, that the ground clave asunder that was under them: And the earth opened her mouth, and swallowed them up, and their houses, and all the men that appertained unto Korah, and all their goods. They, and all that appertained to them, went down alive into the pit, and the earth closed upon them: and they perished from among the congregation. And all Israel that were round about them fled at the cry of them: for they said, Lest the earth swallow us up also. And there came out a fire from the Lord, and consumed the two hundred and fifty men that offered incense. And the Lord spake unto Moses, saying, Speak unto Eleazar the son of Aaron the priest, that he take up the censers out of the burning, and scatter thou the fire yonder; for they are hallowed. The censers of these sinners against their own souls, let them make them broad plates for a covering of the altar: for they offered them before the Lord, therefore they are hallowed: and they shall be a sign unto the children of Israel. And Eleazar the priest took the brasen censers, wherewith they that were burnt had offered; and they were made broad plates for a covering of the altar: To be a memorial unto the children of Israel, that no stranger, which is not of the seed of Aaron, come near to offer incense before the LORD; that he be not as Korah, and as his company: as the LORD said to him by the hand of Moses. But on the morrow all the congregation of the children of Israel murmured against Moses and against Aaron, saying, Ye have killed the people of the LORD. And it came to pass, when the congregation was gathered against Moses and against Aaron, that they looked toward the tabernacle of the congregation: and, behold, the cloud covered it, and the glory of the LORD appeared. And Moses and Aaron came before the tabernacle of the congregation. And the LORD spake unto Moses, saying, Get you up from among this congregation, that I may consume them as in a moment. And they fell upon their faces. And Moses said unto Aaron, Take a censer, and put fire therein from off the altar, and put on incense, and go quickly unto the congregation, and make an atonement for them: for there is wrath gone out from the LORD; the plague is begun. And Aaron took as Moses commanded, and ran into the midst of the congregation; and, behold, the plague was begun among the people: and he put on incense, and made an atonement for the people. And he stood between the dead and the living; and the plague was stayed. Now they that died in the plague were fourteen thousand and seven hundred, beside them that died about the matter of Korah. And Aaron returned unto Moses unto the door of the tabernacle of the congregation: and the plague was stayed.

Numbers 16:1–50 (KJV)

Korah means bald (no covering; rebellion – wanting to do it yourself and have no authority over you). This is a true account of what happened, yet the name Korah is significant and a warning to us when we desire to walk in our own understanding and not be submissive to God and those He puts over us. There will always be someone in authority over us, and we must recognize that God has put them there. God's kingdom is not a democracy!

He is the king, and He has a structure for ruling that doesn't look like ours and doesn't make sense to the natural mind and our cultural conditioning.

The background to this account is that God had assigned Aaron and his sons to be priest and any others who neared the Holy of Holies would die.

> And thou shalt give the Levites unto Aaron and to his sons: they are wholly given unto him out of the children of Israel. And thou shalt appoint Aaron and his sons, and they shall wait on their priest's office: and the stranger that cometh nigh shall be put to death.
>
> Numbers 3:9–10 (KJV)

He gave the sons of Kohath (Korah being lineage of Kohath) other tabernacle duties. Yet they came up to Moses and questioned his authority, saying the entire congregation was holy. Have we ever said or thought, "Who are they to say; we are all kings and priests?" Yes, but God places all of us under authority, and His order always sets up leaders—the fivefold ministry gifts of apostle, prophet, evangelist, pastor, and teachers—for the equipping of the church.

The sons of Korah took the incense and went in presumptuously. Korah and those with him were all swallowed up by an earthquake. The Bible says that they sinned against their own souls (Num. 16:38), but their censors were beaten into plates to hold incense for others. The point of their sin became the means of atonement for others. God will use the point of our sin to save others, once we are corrected and stay in His path.

I believe the lesson for us from the rebellion of Korah is twofold: (1) we must not presume greater authority or position than what God gives us; (2) we must only do exactly what God says—spoken through His appointed leaders. This can also be seen through the example of Miriam and Aaron's rebellion against Moses, in a subsequent section.

Presumption is pride, thinking that we know as much as God, wanting to be our own god (the original temptation to sin). This is how Satan fell from heaven, in his pride presuming he should receive the glory due unto God, and caused Eve to fall by saying she could be like God and God was trying to keep that from them. The temptation is age-old and will continue to tempt us in every area—"Did God say?" We may perceive it differently, "I know best" or "There's nothing wrong with doing this," but in effect we are saying that God is a liar, doubting His word and authority over us; again, wanting to be our own god.

It is dangerous to judge our leaders by our own standards. Korah and his company were judging Moses because they were angry at being in the wilderness so long. We want to blame leaders rather than take responsibility for where we are. They looked at his humanity, forgetting He was appointed by God, and didn't think he was capable of taking them to the Promised Land. Their minds were focused on remembering the food of Egypt—centered on the natural, sensory, and immediate. They were lacking faith and forgetting that God had delivered them out of bondage. They said Moses was trying to make himself a prince. In fact, they were trying to make themselves priests. God had just told them—if you do anything presumptuously, you'll be cut off:

> But the soul that doeth ought presumptuously, whether he be born in the land, or a stranger, the same reproacheth the LORD; and that soul shall be cut off from among his people. Because he hath despised the word of the LORD, and hath broken his commandment, that soul shall utterly be cut off; his iniquity shall be upon him.
>
> Numbers 15:30–31 (KJV)

He also told them to remember His commandments and not to seek after their own heart and their own eyes:

> Speak unto the children of Israel, and bid them that they make them fringes in the borders of their garments

> throughout their generations, and that they put upon the
> fringe of the borders a ribband of blue: And it shall be unto
> you for a fringe, that ye may look upon it, and remember all
> the commandments of the LORD, and do them; and that
> ye seek not after your own heart and your own eyes, after
> which ye use to go a whoring: That ye may remember, and
> do all my commandments, and be holy unto your God. I
> am the LORD your God, which brought you out of the land
> of Egypt, to be your God: I am the LORD your God.
>
> Numbers 15:38–41 (KJV)

The color blue represents heaven and authority. We are to keep in the forefront of our vision the reality of heaven and the spiritual authority of God. We are spirit, soul, and body—first, spirit. Heaven is our true home, and God is our Father. Yet our hearts are prone to wander when we are not looking at things spiritually. We see the natural and forget that God is in control and teaching us along the way as we journey to the land of His promises fulfilled.

> Hear instruction, and be wise, and refuse it not. Blessed
> is the man that heareth me, watching daily at my gates,
> waiting at the posts of my doors. For whoso findeth me
> findeth life, and shall obtain favour of the LORD. But he
> that sinneth against me wrongeth his own soul: all they
> that hate me love death.
>
> Proverbs 8:33–36 (KJV)

They sinned against their own souls because their own souls recognized God and the covenant they had made to follow after God and love him with their whole heart, yet they followed their flesh and pride rather than obey the words of God.

We read in Psalms 12: 6 that the words of the Lord are pure, purified seven times, like silver tried in the fire. Seven is the number of perfection. The Word of God is purified in us until it is perfected. I believe that the purity of the Word is the gold Jesus speaks of in Revelation 3:18 that we are to buy from Him. Gold tried in the fire—the fire of our trials purging everything in us that is contradictory to God's Word.

Pride will cause us to mock authority. Moses's authority was mocked and tested by their desire for status. According to Jude 1:11 (KJV), "Woe to them! For they went the way of Cain, and gave themselves up to the error of Balaam for reward, and perished in the gainsaying of Korah."

Gainsaying, according to Strong's Concordance, means contradiction and/or rebellion.[26] The rebellious spirit in us will not obey the commandments of the Lord because:

1. We don't understand it—it doesn't make sense to our natural mind.

2. Our pride wants to be independent of anyone else telling us what to do.

3. We don't believe God is real and alive now.

4. We don't like anyone having authority over us—we want to be our own god.

Brazen censers (copper/brass) represent sin and judgment. They were to be made into plates to cover the altar. Our sin must be put on the altar so that the sacrifice of Christ can be our atonement. In 1 Corinthians 13, Paul speaks of our words being as sounding brass or tinkling cymbals if we don't have love. Without the love of God in our hearts, everything we say and do has in it motives of self—selfish ambition, self-exaltation, and selfish desires.

They sinned against their own souls (Num. 16:38). Our soul was intended to reflect His glory, but it is a reflection of everything we have put into it. He created us having a soul, but once we are adults, we are responsible for what we put into it. We have the potential of creating our soul to be more like Him, by beholding and acknowledging Him. Bringing our flesh into subjection to the Spirit of Christ creates righteousness in our soul. Listening to the voice of the enemy and the lust of our fleshly desires is what causes us to sin against our own souls.

God said that those who eat of the tree of the knowledge of good and evil will surely die. Questioning God's intention and authority is presuming we know more because of <u>our</u> knowledge of good and evil. This leads to sin and spiritual death. When we have eaten of the tree of the knowledge of good and evil, then we cannot partake of the tree of life. When we repent and turn to Christ, we eat of the tree of life, because He is the tree of life.

Our worship to God rises up to Him as incense. The incense is to be holy unto the Lord, not used for our own purposes (Ex. 30:7–9, 34–38). It will either be sweet, when it is offered up in recognition of who He is, or it will stink, when it rises up from our flesh, seeking our own exaltation or from spiritual lust desiring an experience that makes us feel good. The Bible calls this "strange fire."

> And Nadab and Abihu, the sons of Aaron, took either of them his censer, and put fire therein, and put incense thereon, and offered strange fire before the LORD, which he commanded them not. And there went out fire from the LORD, and devoured them, and they died before the LORD. Then Moses said unto Aaron, This is it that the LORD spake, saying, I will be sanctified in them that come nigh me, and before all the people I will be glorified. And Aaron held his peace.
>
> Leviticus 10:1–3 (KJV)

> And Aaron shall burn thereon sweet incense every morning: when he dresseth the lamps, he shall burn incense upon it. And when Aaron lighteth the lamps at even, he shall burn incense upon it, a perpetual incense before the LORD throughout your generations. Ye shall offer no strange incense thereon, nor burnt sacrifice, nor meat offering; neither shall ye pour drink offering thereon.
>
> Exodus 30:7–9 (KJV)

"Strange fire" means to turn aside, to be foreign or profane. Profane means showing contempt or irreverence toward God or sacred things. They had been clearly warned that those things that are holy unto the Lord are not to be used for their (our) own purposes. (Wow, what about our mouths and our worship, our vessels, which were made by Him to bring honor to Him?)

God Himself brought an end to the questioning of who has authority; God honored Moses's words when he spoke about God sending him, and prophesied the "new thing" of the earth opening its mouth and swallowing up those rebelling against his authority. Two hundred fifty died from the rebellion of Korah and his company, yet the people continued murmuring, this time complaining about the 250 that died. Murmurings bring the wrath of God:

> But on the next day all the congregation of the sons of Israel murmured against Moses and against Aaron saying, You have killed the people of Jehovah.
>
> Numbers 16:41 (NKJV)

> And Moses said to Aaron, Take a fire-pan, and put fire in it from the altar, and put on incense, and go quickly to the congregation and make an atonement for them. For wrath has gone out from Jehovah. The plague has begun.
>
> Numbers 16:46 (NKJV)

The murmuring about these deaths brought the deaths of another 14,700. Is it possible that much of the problems in our lives have been brought about because of our murmurings? And perhaps many of our murmurings stem from our wrong presumptions? Shocking thoughts!

## *Shocking: God's Reputation Is More Important Than Yours*

Looking at the lives of Moses, Saul, Nebucchadnezzer, and Herod, we can see that God deems his reputation more important than ours. Leaders are held highly accountable to glorifying God, to represent Him rightly, as God Himself put them into positions of authority. As leaders, they have great influence on many others.

### MOSES

> And the LORD spake unto Moses that selfsame day, saying, Get thee up into this mountain Abarim, unto mount Nebo, which is in the land of Moab, that is over against Jericho; and behold the land of Canaan, which I give unto the children of Israel for a possession: And die in the mount whither thou goest up, and be gathered unto thy people; as Aaron thy brother died in mount Hor, and was gathered unto his people: Because ye trespassed against me among the children of Israel at the waters of Meribah-Kadesh, in the wilderness of Zin; because ye sanctified me not in the midst of the children of Israel. Yet thou shalt see the land before thee; but thou shalt not go thither unto the land which I give the children of Israel.
>
> Deuteronomy 32:48–52 (KJV)

Moses was God's representative to the people. He spoke for God to them. When Moses reacted in anger and frustration from the people's constant complaining, he did not listen accurately to what God told him to do and reacted in the flesh. Further elaboration on this event is in other sections: (1) "Leaders Are Held to a Higher Accountability," (2) "God Wants to Give Us His Sight Where We Have Blind Spots," and (3) "God Cares about His Name; He Will Be Acclaimed, Not Defamed."

God's reputation is more important than yours. He loves us, and desires relationship with us, but the relationship must be on

His terms. He is God, He is Holy, and He created us for a purpose. Yes, the gifts and callings are without repentance (Rom. 11:29), but God will not give His glory to another (Isa. 42:8). God will not change His mind about the gifts He has given us, but when we try to use them for our own glory, they will not bring about the desired result, or they will destroy us because of our character defects. We can see how many strongly gifted leaders in the church God used mightily, and then they fell to moral indiscretions or character defects (seeking fame, money, abuse of others, etc.). What happened to the people that were touched mightily by the anointing upon these leaders when they saw the same man or woman fall into error? We have seen churches fall apart and people who had been touched mightily scattered because the leaders had been placed up on pedestals they never should have been on.

We know that God will work all things together for good to those who love Him and are called according to His purposes (Rom. 8:28), but it is very harmful to the Body of Christ, and to the world needing to see Him, when leaders fall. It is so easy to be deceived, by refusing to listen to the still, small voice of God when He counsels. When we turn a deaf ear to the Holy Spirit's guidance, the voice of our own flesh and the enemy becomes louder, bringing confusion and doubt to our lives.

Is there anything in your life that you are not allowing His light to touch? Is there an area that you are hiding from others? Are there dark secrets or hidden desires? Have you been seeking and/or listening to ungodly counsel? Does your mind come up with justifications and rationalizations for the choices you are making? Are you flirting with thoughts and actions that have caused problems in the past? Is the Holy Spirit bringing remembrance of similar situations? Is God counseling you in your dreams? Are there situations in others' lives that are similar to yours that He is bringing to your attention, showing you the end result of the error of your thinking? He is trying to show you that you are on a slippery slope, in a danger zone (Jeremiah 13:16). Pay attention! Wide is the gate and broad is the way that leads to destruction, and many there are who go in through it; narrow is the gate and tight is the way that leads to life, and there are few who find it (Matt. 7:13–14).

I can't tell you how many times I can see, in retrospect, God was speaking to me, trying to guide me and keep me on the right path when I was hell-bent on getting my desires met. I also can't tell you how many times I judged others for falling; now I have more compassion for weakness and understand, "There but for the Grace of God go I." I'm hoping someone reading this book will have their understanding of God's ways enlarged so, perhaps, they may not have to learn everything the hard way.

## SAUL

God had anointed Saul to be king, but when he was not obedient, the kingdom was lost to him. He was more concerned about saving face in front of the people than being right with God (1 Samuel, chapters 13–15).

Saul's fall did not happen overnight. It began with impatience, not waiting seven days for Samuel as he had been told to do. He reverted to human reasoning and was told that his kingdom would not endure. Men and women of God, if you are called to leadership, you must be obedient to Him or your leadership will be given to another! We cannot rely on our own reasoning. He desires to bring His people to a place we have not been before— there is no way human reasoning can get us there because human reasoning is based on our own knowledge and experience. Yet God, in His mercy, gave Saul another chance. He was told to destroy the Amelekites—all of them, including the animals. But Saul spared the best. He rationalized his acts by saying that the people wanted the animals for sacrificing to God.

This is the spirit of religion: self-exaltation in rebelling against God to deify tradition. Samuel responds by saying that obedience is better than sacrifice and that rebellion is as the sin of witchcraft (1 Sam. 15:22–23). Saul was then told that he would be cut off completely. What was Saul's response? Recognizing he was disobedient, he still wanted to save face in front of the people by asking Samuel to honor him. The result of Saul's rebellious spirit led to disobedience, self-deception, self-exaltation, and demonic control. He was tormented by evil spirits (1 Sam. 16:14–16) and was bent on murdering David, his successor. The spirit of rebellion against God's authority, if unchecked, will ultimately end up with desire to murder God's people and purposes. The spirit of witchcraft, divination, and Jezebel portray the spirit of religion that deifies self, working manipulation, and control to undermine God's purposes. All stem from the satanic principle of self-deification.

# NEBUCHADNEZZER

This is the interpretation, O king, and this is the decree of the most High, which is come upon my lord the king: That they shall drive thee from men, and thy dwelling shall be with the beasts of the field, and they shall make thee to eat grass as oxen, and they shall wet thee with the dew of heaven, and seven times shall pass over thee, till thou know that the most High ruleth in the kingdom of men, and giveth it to whomsoever he will. And whereas they commanded to leave the stump of the tree roots; thy kingdom shall be sure unto thee, after that thou shalt have known that the heavens do rule. Wherefore, O king, let my counsel be acceptable unto thee, and break off thy sins by righteousness, and thine iniquities by shewing mercy to the poor; if it may be a lengthening of thy tranquillity. All this came upon the king Nebuchadnezzar. At the end of twelve months he walked in the palace of the kingdom of Babylon. The king spake, and said, Is not this great Babylon, that I have built for the house of the kingdom by the might of my power, and for the honour of my majesty? While the word was in the king's mouth, there fell a voice from heaven, saying, O king Nebuchadnezzar, to thee it is spoken; The kingdom is departed from thee. And they shall drive thee from men, and thy dwelling shall be with the beasts of the field: they shall make thee to eat grass as oxen, and seven times shall pass over thee, until thou know that the most High ruleth in the kingdom of men, and giveth it to whomsoever he will. The same hour was the thing fulfilled upon Nebuchadnezzar: and he was driven from men, and did eat grass as oxen, and his body was wet with the dew of heaven, till his hairs were grown like eagles' feathers, and his nails like birds' claws. And at the end of the days I Nebuchadnezzar lifted up mine eyes unto heaven, and mine understanding returned unto me, and I blessed the most High, and I praised and honoured him that liveth for ever, whose dominion is an everlasting dominion, and his kingdom is from generation to generation: And all the inhabitants of the earth are reputed as nothing: and he doeth according to his will in the army of heaven, and among the inhabitants of the earth: and none can stay his hand, or say unto him, What doest thou? At the same time my reason returned unto me; and for the glory of my kingdom, mine honour and brightness returned unto me; and my counsellors and my lords sought unto me; and I was established in my kingdom, and excellent majesty was added unto me. Now I Nebuchadnezzar praise and extol and honour the King of heaven, all whose works are truth, and his ways judgment: and those that walk in pride he is able to abase.

Daniel 4:24–37 (KJV)

Wow, what a story. It is a fearful thing to fall into the hands of the Living God (Hebrews 10:31). Yes, He will raise up leaders for His purposes and how easy it is to begin to think you have done it yourself, once you stop relying on God and rely on the gifts He has given you, thinking they are yours. Many fall after they have become successful in the thing God brought them into, because they forget that He brought them there. He has His ways to bring pride low.

# HEROD

> And upon a set day Herod, arrayed in royal apparel, sat upon his throne, and made an oration unto them. And the people gave a shout, saying, It is the voice of a god, and not of a man. And immediately the angel of the Lord smote him, because he gave not God the glory: and he was eaten of worms, and gave up the ghost.
>
> Acts 12:21–23 (KJV)

Whoa! This needs no elaboration or explanation. In the New Testament too! Clearly, this matters to God. Scripture doesn't tell us that having John the Baptist beheaded was the cause of his death, but that it was a result of his not giving God the glory. For shock value, I can't think of a stronger example.

## *Shocking: Leaders Are Held to a Higher Accountability*

Leaders are held accountable for how they portray God to those He has sent them to lead—He must be seen as Holy among the people.

Moses had been relying on God. The scene at the rock—he'd been there before and God had told him to strike the rock with the rod. He believed God and struck the rock with the rod. Water gushed out for the people. Here he was again, days later, with the people complaining and accusing him of bringing them out in order to kill them. They had forgotten so quickly that God had delivered them from bondage and had declared to them that He would bring them to the Promised Land. He had parted the Red Sea and destroyed their enemy. He had produced water from the rock, manna from heaven, and quail for meat. Now here they were once again, no water. Moses goes to God and cries out to Him, and this time God tells him to take the rod (his authority) and speak to the rock. Moses struck the rock, not just once, but twice, in anger at the people (Num. 20:9–11). As a leader, Moses needed to deal with his feelings ahead of time, before he addressed the people. The people recognized Moses as God's servant, the representative of God, His spokesman, the one who interceded on their behalf. Reacting in anger to them misrepresented God to them. God said that because Moses did not sanctify God before them, he could not enter into the Promised Land. Moses was shocked in the desert because he was taken out by his anger—he forgot his purpose and lost sight of the vision of the Promised Land. In his flesh, he could not see spiritually and it seems he was not able to hear the new instruction. Does the result seem harsh? After all Moses had done for God?

I believe there are four main lessons from this:

- Lesson one—Thou shalt have no other Gods before Me...this includes self. Pride—the same sin by which Satan fell—whether it takes the form of self-aggrandizement or self-debasement, it is still self-centered, not God-centered.

- Lesson two—Take responsibility and don't blame others. Moses said, "These people...;" Adam said, "The woman...." God holds each of us accountable for our own relationship with Him. Greater still does He hold accountable teachers and leaders (James 3:1, Jer. 23:2).

- Lesson three—When pressed, don't act in the flesh. Cry out to God and He will supply your need (Phil. 4:19).

  It is even more important during those times when you are so pressed you think you don't have time to get before God, that you seek Him for peace and wisdom, for direction, for His grace. What was begun in the Spirit cannot be accomplished in the flesh, yet how often is that exactly what we do? We run ahead of God thinking we know what to do, especially if there are similarities to previous events.

- Lesson four – The most critical lesson of all is to maintain fellowship with God. Listen for His voice; what is His direction right now?

Our tendency as humans, with minds that plan our way, is to remember what worked before. We try to walk in the spirit using our own understanding. God is always working to bring us to a new thing; He wants to do a new thing and be glorified in it. The situations we are in may have some similarities to past experiences, and that knowledge can be used to build our faith, but the new thing God wants to do is reveal and manifest an aspect of Himself not hitherto seen. He is infinite, limitless, and unfathomable. His brilliance is unsurpassed. He wanted to have Moses speak to the rock, to exercise authority, dominion over the natural. Moses relied on his previous experience; though spiritual at the time experienced, later it became a work of the flesh—it was not the new thing God wanted to do. This is the gravest danger—becoming complacent in our walk with God, and it is the reason keeping fellowship with Him is the most critical. Jesus said we can do nothing unless we abide in Him. "Abide in me, and I in you. As the branch cannot bear fruit of itself, except it abide in the vine; no more can ye, except ye abide in me" (John 15:4).

Abide in this instance, according to Strong's Concordance, means to stay (in a given place, state, relation or expectancy).[27] Abiding means to stay in a place of expectancy before the Lord. Let that revelation shock you into "now" faith. If we are in the flesh, we are in sense and reason without the Holy Spirit. In the flesh, we are governed by our senses and our mental reasoning. It isn't a stretch to say that if we are angry, anxious, nervous, fearful, even excited in a good way, it is flesh and not Holy Spirit. If we are abiding in Him, in expectancy that He will guide us by Holy Spirit, we will be calm, at peace, able to discern God's voice. This is where the presence of the Lord is and where we will find direction and hear His voice. We cannot hear when we are over-whelmed with agitating passions, good or bad.

Leaders especially must be careful to take the time to be alone with God and get His direction, expecting to see the result of obedience to Him. Scripture indicates that Jesus often went off by himself to pray all night. When God places leaders in authority, they must lead by His authority. In order to do that, they must spend time before Him and go forth in obedient expectancy, or they will end up leading in their own understanding and not seeing the spiritual manifestation God desires to bring forth.

## *Shocking: God Cares about His Name; He Will Be Acclaimed, Not Defamed*

God will always show Himself as holy—He cannot be otherwise. If there is something in us that hinders His being sanctified in us (His holiness being produced through our trials as we turn to Him), it will be removed, and we will be reproved. God will not be defamed; He will be acclaimed. This is especially true for those in leadership, because they impact so many. The gift of leadership causes others to follow, whether or not they are following the truth. Those who have the spiritual gift to lead will be accountable for what they are leading people into. The Word has many scriptures on shepherds being accountable and having a harsh judgment against them when they don't lead with God's heart and direction (Isa. 56:11; Jer. 25:34–36; Jer. 50:6; Ezek. 34:2–10; Nah. 3:18).

God showed up in glory to Moses and Aaron, when they hadn't even requested anything, because He had a purpose—to do a new thing. He told Moses exactly what to do—"Speak to the Rock after gathering the congregation, and before their eyes, it shall give forth HIS water" (Num. 20:8).

> And the LORD spake unto Moses, saying, Take the rod, and gather thou the assembly together, thou, and Aaron

thy brother, and speak ye unto the rock before their eyes; and it shall give forth his water, and thou shalt bring forth to them water out of the rock: so thou shalt give the congregation and their beasts drink. And Moses took the rod from before the LORD, as he commanded him. And Moses and Aaron gathered the congregation together before the rock, and he said unto them, Hear now, ye rebels; must we fetch you water out of this rock? And Moses lifted up his hand, and with his rod he smote the rock twice: and the water came out abundantly, and the congregation drank, and their beasts also. And the LORD spake unto Moses and Aaron, Because ye believed me not, to sanctify me in the eyes of the children of Israel, therefore ye shall not bring this congregation into the land which I have given them. This is the water of Meribah; because the children of Israel strove with the LORD, and he was sanctified in them.

Numbers 20:7–13 (KJV)

Note that He says He will be "sanctified in the EYES of the people" (the perception, the new way of seeing Him) versus "sanctified in the people." There is a difference in the internal process of sanctification by the Spirit versus seeing Him as sanctified, Holy before our eyes. By Moses striking the rock as he had done before, they saw that God was able and did provide water for their needs, but they didn't get to see it done by Moses speaking the Word only in the authority that God desired him to use. Had he spoken as commanded, the people would have seen the new level of authority and the creative power of speaking the Word of God in faith. In comparison, when the people finally made it to the edge of the Promised Land, only those who spoke the right thing were able to enter in. Those entering in spoke words of faith—trusting in God's word that it was a good land and He was giving it to them. What we speak is important to God. "Promised" in Strong's Concordance means to say, answer, appoint; avouch; talk, use speech, utter.[28] God spoke it as a promise; we must speak it in faith, believing Him!

God being misrepresented from the pulpit, that is, not recognizing what He is doing in the circumstances and blaming Satan or others, will not be tolerated. God will not be defamed. He will be seen as Holy. If you are in leadership, God has placed you there, and He must be rightly represented to the people through you. If you do not hallow Him before the people, He will not allow you to remain in the high position where He has placed you. You will be shocked. God is not like us.

Hear these words that Moses spoke later:

> Give ear, O heavens, and I will speak; and hear, O earth, the words of my mouth. My doctrine shall drop as the rain; my speech shall drop down as the dew, as the small rain on the tender plant, and as the showers on the grass; because I will proclaim the name of Jehovah, ascribe greatness to our God. He is the Rock; His work is perfect. For all His ways are just, a God of faithfulness, and without evil; just and upright is He.
>
> Deuteronomy 32:1–4 (NKJV)

Consider; this he spoke after being told he would die and not cross the Jordan (Num. 20:12; Deut. 34:1–6). The people knew this. Many would probably be offended. Moses could have been offended! Yet Moses had learned of God's perfect judgment, His Holiness; that every word that is spoken by the mouth of the Lord is true and effectual; that there is life, redemption, deliverance, and provision in Him; that we are utterly dependent on Him if we are to secure the fullness of the promises. He knew that God is holy and just, and that he deserved the consequences of his disobedience and reacting in the flesh, not hallowing God before the people.

Moses learned, at the rock, that Jesus is the rock that would give forth His water. Moses smote the rock twice, in the anger of his flesh at the people, but also at his frustration in having to lead them. He did not recognize the importance of following explicit instruction, as God told him to speak to the rock. Jesus is the rock; He has already been smitten, before the foundation of the world (1 Pet. 1:18–20; Rev. 13:7–8)! When we react in the flesh in situations in our lives, we are smiting Him again. God wants us to take the authority given us through Jesus's death, burial, and resurrection, and speak to our situations to bring His will and presence, glorifying Him before the people in our lives.

Moses was to speak to the rock. Jesus is the rock and the fount of living water. Jesus said if we tell the mountain to move, it will move.

> Jesus answered and said unto them, Verily I say unto you, If ye have faith, and doubt not, ye shall not only do this which is done to the fig tree, but also if ye shall say unto this mountain, Be thou removed, and be thou cast into the sea; it shall be done.
>
> Matthew 21:21 (KJV)

Jesus was struck on the cross and now the water of His spirit flows freely in us. As we have drunk from the rock, we have the ability to speak through this relationship—He is in us. The rod symbolizes the authority of Christ—given by God to us—having received of His Spirit. Now we can speak to the rock for provision. Natural resources, and spiritual, are under His lordship. When Moses asked to see His Glory, God told him to stand upon a rock, and when the Glory passed by, He would put him in a "cleft" of the rock, and cover him with his hand. Cleft, according to Strong's Concordance, means to bore, penetrate, and pierce.[29] He was pierced for our transgressions. As we are hidden in Him, standing on the rock of His strength and authority, we will see Him move—after He moves by we will know He has been there. We usually are not aware of God's movement until afterward, as we reflect on what transpired.

God was angry with Moses because Moses did not allow God to be sanctified through him. God desires to be sanctified in and through us. When He is hallowed in us is when others will know He is God.

> And I will sanctify my great name, which was profaned among the heathen, which ye have profaned in the midst of them; and the heathen shall know that I am the LORD, saith the LORD GOD, when I shall be sanctified in you before their eyes.
>
> Ezekiel 36:23 (KJV)

How do we sanctify the Lord? By recognizing that He is God, He is holy, He is just, and allowing Him to be lord of our lives. As Lord, we obey Him, by faith expecting He will perform, recognizing that He has made us and purposed us for His pleasure (Rev. 4:11). In John 4:34 (KJV), we read, "Jesus saith unto them, My meat is to do the will of Him who sent me and to finish His work." He was always about the Father's business. He knew His purpose, and nothing could deter him. Although He was in the form of God, He made Himself of no reputation, but of a servant, and took upon himself the likeness of a man, humbling Himself in obedience to death on the cross (Phil. 2:5–8).

## REBELLION BEGINS IN THE HEART

> And Moses and Aaron gathered the congregation together before the rock, and he said unto them, Hear now, ye rebels; must we fetch you water out of this rock?
>
> Numbers 20:10 (KJV)

> And the LORD spake unto Moses and Aaron in mount Hor, by the coast of the land of Edom, saying, Aaron shall be gathered unto his people: for he shall not enter into the land which I have given unto the children of Israel, because ye rebelled against my word at the water of Meribah. Take Aaron and Eleazar his son, and bring them up unto mount

Hor: And strip Aaron of his garments, and put them upon Eleazar his son: and Aaron shall be gathered unto his people, and shall die there. And Moses did as the LORD commanded: and they went up into mount Hor in the sight of all the congregation. And Moses stripped Aaron of his garments, and put them upon Eleazar his son; and Aaron died there in the top of the mount: and Moses and Eleazar came down from the mount. And when all the congregation saw that Aaron was dead, they mourned for Aaron thirty days, even all the house of Israel.

Numbers 20:23–29 (KJV)

Moses/Aaron had accused the people of being rebels, but God said that they were the rebels! Could it be that the people were manifesting what was in Moses and Aaron's heart? This bears two points. First, godly anointed leaders must always bear in mind that they are representing God to the people and will be held accountable to show them that they are under His authority. Second, we eat from the fruit of our lips. The judgment from speaking forth in anger, calling the people rebels was brought back upon Aaron (and Moses, later). Speak in judgment, receive judgment.

Jesus warns us in Matthew 7:1 and Luke 6:37 to judge not, that we be not judged. This is not that God is punitive; it is because He has given us creative ability—we are the ones creating the judgment upon ourselves. Before we speak, we need to check the condition of our heart before God. If we are tired of the burdens we are bearing, we need to take them before Him and lay it at His feet prior to representing Him before the people. Whatever is in our heart is going to come out of our mouth, and we will eat the fruit of it. Rebellion is as witchcraft, and stubbornness as iniquity and idolatry, according to 1 Samuel 15:23. What is the source of our heart position? It is critical to ascertain that before we represent God to others. Are we speaking for Him or have we allowed the enemy to plant seeds of bitterness in our hearts?

# DISCOURAGEMENT LEADS TO DISAPPOINTMENT; WHEN YOU "DIS" COURAGE, YOU WILL "DIS" YOUR APPOINTED TIME

And they journeyed from Mount Hor by the way of the Red Sea, to compass the land of Edom: and the soul of the people was much discouraged because of the way. And the people spake against God, and against Moses, Wherefore have ye brought us up out of Egypt to die in the wilderness? for there is no bread, neither is there any water; and our soul loatheth this light bread. And the LORD sent fiery serpents among the people, and they bit the people; and much people of Israel died. Therefore the people came to Moses, and said, We have sinned, for we have spoken against the LORD, and against thee; pray unto the LORD, that he take away the serpents from us. And Moses prayed for the people. And the LORD said unto Moses, Make thee a fiery serpent, and set it upon a pole: and it shall come to pass, that every one that is bitten, when he looketh upon it, shall live. And Moses made a serpent of brass, and put it upon a pole, and it came to pass, that if a serpent had bitten any man, when he beheld the serpent of brass, he lived.

Numbers 21:4–9 (KJV)

The soul of the people was discouraged. "Discourage" in Strong's Concordance means to dock off, that is, curtail (transitively or intransitively, literally or figuratively); especially to harvest (grass or grain).[30] "Loatheth" in Strong's Concordance is similar, indicating a severing oneself from; to abhor, be distressed, be grieved, loathe, vex, be weary.[31]

The people were impatient with the journey and the trials they were experiencing and became discouraged, which in effect means that they cut themselves off from their harvest! Critical lesson! How imperative that we recognize that God is always with us, guiding us, and that He will provide for our needs, and is in fact providing for our needs all the time. If we react impatiently, we cut ourselves off from the blessing that is coming!

They called the bread from heaven worthless, and said they loathed it! What was the result? Their words caused them to be anxious, grieved, vexed and brought immediate judgment: fiery serpents; the fiery darts of the enemy, whether it is in vexing thoughts, plaguing problems, sickness, irritations—ending in death, should we not recognize what is happening and repent.

## GOOD NEWS! OUR FAILURES BRING US TO THE CROSS

And as Moses lifted up the serpent in the wilderness, even so must the Son of man be lifted up: That whosoever believeth in him should not perish, but have eternal life. For God so loved the world, that he gave his only begotten Son, that whosoever believeth in him should not perish, but have everlasting life. For God sent not his Son into the world to condemn the world; but that the world through him might be saved.

John 3:14–17 (KJV)

Oh, the beauty of the cross: Jesus Christ himself taking our punishment; if we look upon Him–the way, the truth and the life–we shall live. We must look upon the Lord Jesus and be saved. To look upon is more than mentally assent to knowledge. It means to behold, perceive, consider, regard, discern, respect, to advise self. There is an awareness of position of self, actions and mindsets held that have brought us to this place, and a subsequent change of mind, recognizing our sin, our rebellion against God, and desiring to come back to that rightful place of humility, thankfulness and adoration. How often after we have been on the faith journey many years, that His blessings become commonplace to us, we "loathe" where we are and are no longer grateful. The serpent of brass is a reminder of our sin and that it has been put upon Jesus, on the cross. He was made sin for us, that we might have His life in its stead. God will be acclaimed, whether by being glorified through our obedience or through His judgment on our sin. Thank God for the cross – we can ever repent and come before Him as long as we have breath in our body.

## *Shocking: Put God to the Test, You Don't Get to Enter His Rest*

God said that because they provoked Him, putting Him to the test (due to erring hearts), they would not enter into His rest. In the books of Numbers, Deuteronomy, and Exodus, we see that He says they shall not enter the Promised Land.

The Promised Land is the land of rest—resting in Him, trusting Him to not just provide for our needs but to bless us with every heavenly and natural blessing. He is the God of all, and He is our Heavenly Father—we have been reconciled to our original relationship with our Father through the blood of Christ shed for us. We now have our inheritance restored to us and can walk in His blessings, one with Him in every moment, listening to His voice directing us to see His kingdom manifested in our lives.

> So then there remains a rest to the people of God. For he who has entered into his rest, he also has ceased from his own works, as God did from His. Therefore let us labor to enter into that rest, lest anyone fall after the same example of unbelief.
>
> Hebrews 4:9–11 (NKJV)

His Kingdom is now, here, if we believe. His promised land already exists. We labor to enter that rest—the place where we believe—where we see spiritually, seeing Him ever before us, not seeing the natural, but seeing His provision, kingdom promises realized, the fullness of Him who fills all in all. The labor is pressing through our mindsets, our fleshly desires, and the hindering spirits that war against us to keep us from entering fully into the mind of

Christ. We must labor against unbelief, doubt and complacency, to stir ourselves up so that we are full of faith in what He has promised!

> Oh come, let us worship and bow down; let us kneel before Jehovah our maker. For He is our God, and we are the people of His pasture, and the sheep of His hand. Today if you will hear His voice, harden not your heart, as in the day of strife, as in the day of testing in the wilderness; when your fathers tempted Me, tested Me, and saw My work. For forty years I was grieved with this generation, and said, It is a people who go astray in their hearts, and they have not known My ways; to whom I swore in My wrath that they should not enter into My rest.
>
> Psalms 95:6–11 (NKJV)

> You shall not tempt Jehovah your God as you tempted in Massah. You shall carefully keep the commandments of Jehovah your God, and His testimonies, and His statutes which He has commanded you. And you shall do the right and good in the sight of Jehovah, so that it may be well with you, and so that you may go in and possess the good land which Jehovah swore to your fathers, to cast out all your enemies from before you, as Jehovah has spoken.
>
> Deuteronomy 6:16–19 (NKJV)

> But truly, as I live, all the earth shall be filled with the glory of Jehovah. Because all those men who have seen My glory and My miracles which I did in Egypt and in the wilderness, and have tempted Me now these ten times, and have not listened to My voice, surely they shall not see the land which I swore to their fathers, neither shall any of them that provoked Me see it. But My servant Caleb, because he had another spirit with him, and has followed Me fully, I will bring him into the land into which he went. And his seed shall possess it.
>
> Numbers 14:21–24 (NKJV)

> Wherefore the people did chide with Moses, and said, Give us water that we may drink. And Moses said unto them, Why chide ye with me? wherefore do ye tempt the LORD? And the people thirsted there for water; and the people murmured against Moses, and said, Wherefore is this that thou hast brought us up out of Egypt, to kill us and our children and our cattle with thirst?
>
> Exodus 17:2–3 (KJV)

Chide, according to Strong's Concordance, means to toss, grabble, and hold a controversy to defend complaining, contending, debating, adversary.[32] The people were questioning God's goodness, motives, and purposes. This is provoking God. He had shown them His goodness over and over, and they still didn't believe He was good. If we aren't walking in faith, resting in the reality of what Christ finished on the cross, are we any less provoking to Him? These people do "err in heart," Paul says in the letter to the Hebrews (Heb. 3:10 KJV). Err is to cause to roam from safety, virtue or truth; to go astray, seduce, and deceive, according to Strong's Concordance.[33]

"But my servant Caleb, because he had another spirit with him, and hath followed me fully, him will I bring into the land whereinto he went; and his seed shall possess it" (Num. 14:24 KJV). Caleb had another spirit and followed God fully. Only he and Joshua would enter. The others gave an evil report, according to Numbers 14:32. Interestingly, evil in this statement of evil report is the same word as slander in Numbers 14:36, according to Strong's Concordance.[34]

> And the men, which Moses sent to search the land, who returned, and made all the congregation to murmur against him, by bringing up a slander upon the land, Even those men that did bring up the evil report upon the land, died by the plague before the LORD.
>
> Numbers 14:36–37 (KJV)

According to Strong's Concordance, slander means defaming and infamy; to cause to speak furtively.[35] In the dictionary, defaming means attacking the good name; infamy means evil fame or reputation; furtively means suggesting hidden motives or purposes, being shifty. The people murmured against God attributing evil intentions to Him! God said in response:

> Say unto them, "As truly as I live, saith the LORD, as ye have spoken in mine ears, so will I do to you: Your carcasses shall fall in this wilderness; and all that were numbered of you, according to your whole number, from twenty years old and upward, which have murmured against me,"
>
> Numbers 14:28–29 (KJV)

God always punishes sin against His Name. He is good, always, and the purpose of our lives is to bring glory to His Name. If we are speaking inherent evil about Him, we are causing evil to come into our lives. He is good. Our words bring manifestation—what are we saying? What is the truth in our hearts, being brought out in our lips? If we err in our hearts, let us confess that to God and ask Him to cleanse us, to unite our heart to fear His name. Open our eyes, Lord. Shock us back to reality, to see you as you are. Let us be shocked now, for a moment, rather than for eternity shocked that we lived our lives blindly seeking after momentary fleshly fulfillment yet as walking dead men, empty of soul. Open our eyes to see your springs of water right here, waiting for us to come and drink.

## Shocking: Dishonoring Authority Is Treasonous to God (God Honors Those He Puts in Authority)

> And Miriam and Aaron spake against Moses because of the Ethiopian woman whom he had married: for he had married an Ethiopian woman. And they said, Hath the LORD

indeed spoken only by Moses? hath he not spoken also by us? And the LORD heard it. (Now the man Moses was very meek, above all the men which were upon the face of the earth.) And the LORD spake suddenly unto Moses, and unto Aaron, and unto Miriam, Come out ye three unto the tabernacle of the congregation. And they three came out. And the LORD came down in the pillar of the cloud, and stood in the door of the tabernacle, and called Aaron and Miriam: and they both came forth. And he said, Hear now my words: If there be a prophet among you, I the LORD will make myself known unto him in a vision, and will speak unto him in a dream. My servant Moses is not so, who is faithful in all mine house. With him will I speak mouth to mouth, even apparently, and not in dark speeches; and the similitude of the LORD shall he behold: wherefore then were ye not afraid to speak against my servant Moses? And the anger of the LORD was kindled against them; and he departed. And the cloud departed from off the tabernacle; and, behold, Miriam became leprous, white as snow: and Aaron looked upon Miriam, and, behold, she was leprous.

Numbers 12:1–10 (KJV)

Miriam and Aaron spoke against Moses because he'd married an Ethiopian (Cushite), and the result is that Miriam becomes leprous. Ethiopians are darker skinned. The result of Miriam's prejudice against skin color directly resulted in leprosy—a disease of the skin. Shocking—sometimes God's justice results in our judging of others turning directly back upon us. It would do us well to examine areas of our lives where God may be correcting us.

Miriam was a prophetess, used by God to speak to the people. The prophet has a great responsibility to speak rightly because God's creative spirit in them empowers their words to bring forth. (Aaron's rebellion would go further and result in early death as punishment.)

Miriam and Aaron's justification was that God speaks through them also, so why should they listen to Moses? Because God had given Moses authority; He placed Moses in leadership. God, in His chastisement of Miriam and Aaron, addresses the prophet's gifting in relation to the authority given to Moses. Authority given by God takes precedence over gifting. Yes, we should all hear from God, but God raises up those faithful to His purposes, those who put God's purposes above their own desires. God rebuked Miriam and Aaron because they spoke against Moses.

> And he said, Hear now my words: If there be a prophet among you, I the Lord will make myself known unto him in a vision, and will speak unto him in a dream. My servant Moses is not so, who is faithful in all mine house. With him will I speak mouth to mouth, even apparently, and not in dark speeches; and the similitude of the Lord shall he behold: wherefore then were ye not afraid to speak against my servant Moses?
>
> Numbers 12:6–8 (KJV)

According to Strong's Concordance, faithful in this instance means to build up or support; to foster, as a parent or nurse; to render firm, to trust or believe, to be permanent, and to be true.[36] So God is saying to them, here is where Moses is set apart from you—Moses builds up and supports my family; He is trustworthy to my purposes; He is steady and firm in his walk. The emphasis here is that although Moses is also a prophet, as they are arguing, he has been raised up to lead the people because he was found faithful. In the position of leader, God has given him greater authority and should be recognized as such and honored because of his position.

## Shocking: The Earth Itself Speaks Forth the Truth

And Cain talked with Abel his brother: and it came to pass, when they were in the field, that Cain rose up against Abel his brother, and slew him. And the Lord said unto

Cain, Where is Abel thy brother? And he said, I know not: Am I my brother's keeper? And he said, What hast thou done? the voice of thy brother's blood crieth unto me from the ground.

Genesis 4:8–10 (KJV)

All things that are created by God answer to Him, communicate to Him and respond to His voice. There is no place far enough from God to run; all created things are His and responsive to Him.

And Joshua wrote these words in the book of the law of God, and took a great stone, and set it up there under an oak, that was by the sanctuary of the LORD. And Joshua said unto all the people, Behold, this stone shall be a witness unto us; for it hath heard all the words of the LORD which he spake unto us: it shall be therefore a witness unto you, lest ye deny your God.

Joshua 24:26–27 (KJV)

In Luke 19:38–40, we read that Jesus said if we don't praise Him, the stones will cry out! There is a reality beyond what our five senses perceive—the supernatural. The Word of God says that the creation itself bears witness to God (Rom. 1:20). In creation we see His majesty, omnipotence and omniscience, His infinite intelligence and beauty.

So then faith cometh by hearing, and hearing by the word of God. But I say, Have they not heard? Yes verily, their sound went into all the earth, and their words unto the ends of the world.

Romans 10:17–18 (KJV)

The heavens declare the glory of God; and the firmament sheweth his handywork. Day unto day uttereth speech, and night unto night sheweth knowledge. There is no speech nor language, where their voice is not heard. Their line is gone out through all the earth, and their words to the end of the world.

Psalms 19:1–4 (KJV)

The word line in Strong's Concordance means a cord (as connecting), especially for measuring; figuratively a rule; also a rim, a musical string or accord, and comes from a root word meaning to bind together, collect; (figuratively) to expect: gather (together), look, patiently, tarry, wait (for, on, upon).[37]

Did you know, amazingly, that the black hole has sound? It is the sound of B flat, 57 octaves below middle C, a sound that the human ear can't hear. (http://www.nasa.gov/centers/goddard/universe/black_hole_sound.html)

Science has proven that all things that move make sound. We are reverberating throughout the atmosphere, and God hears us. He hears a sparrow fall. He hears the sound of those we harm crying out. He hears us crying out when we are harmed. We were created to bring praise and glory and honor to Him. All of creation is waiting for that day, that grand and glorious day, when the sons of God are manifest and liberty reigns once more—freedom in the spirit; no more guilt, no more shame, for we will be giving glory to His Name.

> The Spirit itself beareth witness with our spirit, that we are the children of God: And if children, then heirs; heirs of God, and joint-heirs with Christ; if so be that we suffer with him, that we may be also glorified together. For I reckon that the sufferings of this present time are not worthy to be compared with the glory which shall be revealed in us. For the earnest expectation of the creature waiteth for the manifestation of the sons of God. For the creature was made subject to vanity, not willingly, but by reason of him who hath subjected the same in hope, Because the creature itself also shall be delivered from the bondage of

corruption into the glorious liberty of the children of God. For we know that the whole creation groaneth and travaileth in pain together until now. And not only they, but ourselves also, which have the first fruits of the Spirit, even we ourselves groan within ourselves, waiting for the adoption, to wit, the redemption of our body.

Romans 8:16–23 (KJV)

What is this redemption of our body? Is it the second coming of Christ, when we are caught up in the air with Him; is it when we see Him face-to-face? Is it when we return with Him and reign with Him in glory?

Interestingly, the Greek words for redemption and body in Romans 8:23 have been translated very loosely, in my opinion. You can make your own conclusions. Here are the Greek definitions from the Strong's Concordance:

Redemption, in Strong's Concordance, indicates ransom paid in full, Christian salvation; deliverance, redemption paid.[38]

Body, in Strong's Concordance, is the body (as a sound whole), and used in a very wide application, literally or figuratively; rooted in the Greek word sōzō which means to save, deliver or protect (literally or figuratively):–heal, preserve, save (self), do well, be (make) whole.[39]

I think that it is very interesting that the word for body literally means sound, whole, healed. We are waiting for the adoption, the redemption of our body that we be made whole. The Bible speaks of being saved to the uttermost (Heb. 7:25), that there is a prosperity for our soul (3 John 1:2), and that our body, soul, and spirit can be preserved blameless (1 Thess. 5:23). I believe that we are called to this, as a great and precious promise; that this is the state of the pure bride without spot or wrinkle that Jesus will be coming to retrieve. He died and paid the price of all sin. We are to walk in divine, resurrection power, manifesting to the world that we are truly the sons of God. This is the rest we can walk in—completely in love and one with Him, not relying on our own works, but listening for His voice, trusting Him and obeying. In this perfect childlike trust, we are fully protected, and all our needs are met. This is a place of perfect submission to the One who has all authority over heaven and earth (Colossians 1:16), recognizing that He is Lord of all (Acts 10:36).

# SHOCKING: THE REALITY OF PROGRESSIVE REVELATION

## *Shocking: God Is Infinite; We Receive Progressive Revelation of Who He Is to Go Forward in Him*

> My servant Moses is not so, who is faithful in all mine house.
> With him will I speak mouth to mouth, even apparently, and
> not in dark speeches; and the similitude of the LORD shall he
> behold: wherefore then were ye not afraid to speak against
> my servant Moses?
>
> Numbers 12:7–8 (KJV)

Similitude in Strong's Concordance means shape, embodiment, image, manifestation.[40] Moses saw the Lord in greater manifestation than anyone else at that time, and received progressive revelation as he walked in faith.

## MOSES RECEIVED REVELATION OF THE LORD AS DELIVERER

Moses was delivered from death just after his birth. God placed a burden on him to deliver his people. At first, Moses tried to be a deliverer in his own flesh, and he killed an Egyptian who was harming a Hebrew. Fear of punishment for murder sent him running out of Egypt for his life.

## MOSES RECEIVED REVELATION AS TO GOD'S DIVINITY

Moses received revelation of God's divinity during his forty years in the wilderness after acting in the flesh, a humbling and necessary experience. It is not in scripture, but I am certain that during his time in his own personal wilderness, he received revelation as to God's holy character, His purpose for Moses and His plan for accomplishing that purpose, the deliverance of His people from bondage, and going forth into the Promised Land.

Psalms 103:7 records that God made His acts known to the children of Israel, but His ways were made known unto Moses. We first learn of God through His actions in our lives. Hopefully, we mature and begin to understand His ways, so that we can make the right choices based on our knowledge of Him rather than being corrected. Knowing someone's ways only happens when there is intimacy, walking with them day by day and taking note of how, when, and why they do things.

> Give ear, O ye heavens, and I will speak; and hear, O earth, the words of my mouth. My doctrine shall drop as the rain, my speech shall distil as the dew, as the small rain upon the tender herb, and as the showers upon the grass: Because I will publish the name of the LORD: ascribe ye greatness unto our God.
>
> Deuteronomy 32:1–3 (KJV)

Moses said, "Because I publish the name of the Lord: ascribe greatness to our God." Moses recognized the greatness of God and his own role to publish, or bear witness to Him. We have already seen that God honored Moses for his faithfulness to build up His family. Moses recognized the divinity of God—His greatness, but also that His doctrine, or Word, goes forth and creates.

Distil in Strong's Concordance means to drip, or shed by trickling.[41] Dew is to cover.[42] Small rain means a tempestuous shower,[43] and the root word for showers is to increase, to multiply by the myriad, tens of thousands.[44]

I believe that this shows us that the doctrine of the Lord by His Word goes forth in many levels. When we are young in the Lord, His Word covers gently, saturating our soul. As we grow it comes in showers upon us and causes turbulence as it uproots those things in opposition. As we have grown stronger in the Lord, we can withstand the harder rain as it falls and not be broken. As mature believers, His Word can then bear fruit in our lives and multiplies in magnitude.

## MOSES RECEIVED REVELATION OF THE LORD AS THE ROCK OF AGES

Moses recognized the Lord as the rock—the fortress, immovable and steadfast, solid in strength. He exhorted the people to leave behind their impotent gods and come to the rock of ages.

> For they are a nation void of counsel, neither is there any understanding in them. O that they were wise, that they understood this, that they would consider their latter end! How should one chase a thousand, and two put ten thousand to flight, except their Rock had sold them, and the LORD had shut them up? For their rock is not as our Rock, even our enemies themselves being judges. For their vine is of the vine of Sodom, and of the fields of Gomorrah: their grapes are grapes of gall, their clusters are bitter:
>
> Deuteronomy 32:28–32 (KJV)

On Mount Sinai, Moses asked to see His glory. The Lord replied that He would go by him and hide him in the cleft of the rock, and that Moses would see His back side, after He passed by.

> And Moses said unto the LORD, See, thou sayest unto me, Bring up this people: and thou hast not let me know whom thou wilt send with me. Yet thou hast said, I know thee by name, and thou hast also found grace in my sight. Now therefore, I pray thee, if I have found grace in thy sight, shew me now thy way, that I may know thee, that I may find grace in thy sight: and consider that this nation is thy people. And he said, My presence shall go with thee, and I will give thee rest. And he said unto him, If thy presence go not with me, carry us not up hence. For wherein shall it be known here

that I and thy people have found grace in thy sight? is it not in that thou goest with us? so shall we be separated, I and thy people, from all the people that are upon the face of the earth. And the LORD said unto Moses, I will do this thing also that thou hast spoken: for thou hast found grace in my sight, and I know thee by name. And the LORD said unto Moses, I will do this thing also that thou hast spoken: for thou hast found grace in my sight, and I know thee by name. And he said, I beseech thee, shew me thy glory.

Exodus 33:12–18 (KJV)

And he said, Thou canst not see my face: for there shall no man see me, and live. And the LORD said, Behold, there is a place by me, and thou shalt stand upon a rock: And it shall come to pass, while my glory passeth by, that I will put thee in a cleft of the rock, and will cover thee with my hand while I pass by: And I will take away mine hand, and thou shalt see my back parts: but my face shall not be seen.

Exodus 33:20–23 (KJV)

Hidden in the cleft of the rock (hidden in Christ) is the only way we can see God (only the pure in heart shall see God; therefore, by His atoning work and our receiving a new heart). We have to stay in the position of humility to continue to see God. Jesus said He only did that which He saw the Father doing.

And the LORD descended in the cloud, and stood with him there, and proclaimed the name of the LORD. And the LORD passed by before him, and proclaimed, The LORD, The LORD God, merciful and gracious, longsuffering, and abundant in goodness and truth, keeping mercy for thousands, forgiving iniquity and transgression and sin, and that will by no means clear the guilty; visiting the iniquity of the fathers upon the children, and upon the children's children, unto the third and to the fourth generation.

Exodus 34:5–7 (KJV)

# MOSES RECEIVED REVELATION OF THE LORD AS MERCIFUL, GRACIOUS, LONG-SUFFERING, ABUNDANT IN GOODNESS AND TRUTH

God showed Moses His glory by proclaiming His nature of mercy and grace, long-suffering toward us. This longsuffering aspect is what Moses would be tested on with the people in those long years in the wilderness. It was His mercy that He desired Moses to show Israel when he failed to allow God to be sanctified in him, at the second smiting of the rock.

> And it came to pass, when Moses came down from mount Sinai with the two tables of testimony in Moses' hand, when he came down from the mount, that Moses wist not that the skin of his face shone while he talked with him.
>
> Exodus 34:29 (KJV)

Moses had clearly been in the glory.

# MOSES RECEIVED REVELATION THAT JESUS IS LORD

Jesus said that Moses wrote of Him and would accuse those who did not believe on Him.

> Do not think that I will accuse you to the Father: there is one that accuseth you, even Moses, in whom ye trust. For had ye believed Moses, ye would have believed me: for he wrote of me. But if ye believe not his writings, how shall ye believe my words?
>
> John 5:45–47 (KJV)

Where did Moses write of Jesus?

> Because I will publish the name of the LORD: ascribe ye
> greatness unto our God. He is the Rock, his work is per-
> fect: for all his ways are judgment: a God of truth and
> without iniquity, just and right is he.
>
> Deuteronomy 32:3–4 (KJV)

## MOSES RECEIVED REVELATION OF JESUS AS LIVING WATER

When Moses struck the rock and water came forth, Moses
received revelation that Jesus is the rock from which we all drink.
To confirm, Paul wrote:

> Moreover, brethren, I would not that ye should be igno-
> rant, how that all our fathers were under the cloud, and all
> passed through the sea; And were all baptized unto Moses
> in the cloud and in the sea; And did all eat the same spir-
> itual meat; And did all drink the same spiritual drink: for
> they drank of that spiritual Rock that followed them: and
> that Rock was Christ.
>
> 1 Corinthians 10:1–4 (KJV)

## MOSES RECEIVED REVELATION OF RESURRECTION AND ETERNAL LIFE

> Now that the dead are raised, even Moses showed at the
> bush, when he calleth the Lord the God of Abraham, and
> the God of Isaac, and the God of Jacob. For he is not a
> God of the dead, but of the living: for all live unto him.
>
> Luke 20:37–38 (KJV)

## MOSES RECEIVED REVELATION OF JESUS AS THE ATONEMENT

In John 3: 14 (KJV), we read, "And as Moses lifted up the serpent in the wilderness, even so must the Son of man be lifted up." John is referring to the following incident:

> And the people spake against God, and against Moses, Wherefore have ye brought us up out of Egypt to die in the wilderness? for there is no bread, neither is there any water; and our soul loatheth this light bread. And the LORD sent fiery serpents among the people, and they bit the people; and much people of Israel died. Therefore the people came to Moses, and said, We have sinned, for we have spoken against the LORD, and against thee; pray unto the LORD, that he take away the serpents from us. And Moses prayed for the people. And the LORD said unto Moses, Make thee a fiery serpent, and set it upon a pole: and it shall come to pass, that every one that is bitten, when he looketh upon it, shall live. And Moses made a serpent of brass, and put it upon a pole, and it came to pass, that if a serpent had bitten any man, when he beheld the serpent of brass, he lived.
>
> Numbers 21:5–9 (KJV)

Brass represents judgment. Moses making a serpent of brass and lifting it up shows that judgment has been made. The pole represents the cross of Christ. As we look upon Him who took upon Himself our sin, we are saved.

## MOSES RECEIVED REVELATION OF JESUS AS COMING KING

> For Moses truly said unto the fathers, A prophet shall the Lord your God raise up unto you of your brethren, like unto me; him shall ye hear in all things whatsoever he shall say unto you. And it shall come to pass, that every soul,

which will not hear that prophet, shall be destroyed from among the people.

Acts 3:22–23 (KJV)

For the testimony of Jesus is the spirit of prophecy (Rev. 19:10). God desires that in our trials we will press in until we see Him glorified in it—a new revelation of an aspect of Jesus that we have not known (1 Pet. 1:13). He is infinite, limitless, unfathomable in the many aspects of His being. He is above finding out, yet He desires that we continue to seek Him and find Him. He desires to be revealed and manifested in our life that others will see Him and be drawn to Him (John 12:52; Rom. 8:18; 1 Pet. 4:13).

## *Shocking: His Sending Sustains Us*

### ELIJAH

Elijah means "my God is Jehovah." After seeing God move mightily by bringing a drought at his word, providing food for him through the ravens, then through the widow, bringing her son back to life, instigating a showdown between God and Baal (where God wins by a landslide and Baal followers are put to shame) and slaying 850 of Jezebel's prophets (prophets of Baal), bringing rain through his faithful prayers, outrunning a chariot when God empowered him, Elijah became afraid when Jezebel threatened to kill him. He ran for his life, leaving his servant at Beer-sheba, and going off himself into the wilderness.

> But he himself went a day's journey into the wilderness, and came and sat down under a juniper tree: and he requested for himself that he might die; and said, It is enough; now, O LORD, take away my life; for I am not better than my fathers. And as he lay and slept under a juniper tree, behold, then an angel touched him, and said unto him, Arise and eat. And he looked, and, behold, there was a cake baken on the coals, and a cruse of water at his

head. And he did eat and drink, and laid him down again. And the angel of the LORD came again the second time, and touched him, and said, Arise and eat; because the journey is too great for thee. And he arose, and did eat and drink, and went in the strength of that meat forty days and forty nights unto Horeb the mount of God. And he came thither unto a cave, and lodged there; and, behold, the word of the LORD came to him, and he said unto him, What doest thou here, Elijah? And he said, I have been very jealous for the LORD God of hosts: for the children of Israel have forsaken thy covenant, thrown down thine altars, and slain thy prophets with the sword; and I, even I only, am left; and they seek my life, to take it away. And he said, Go forth, and stand upon the mount before the LORD. And, behold, the LORD passed by, and a great and strong wind rent the mountains, and brake in pieces the rocks before the LORD; but the LORD was not in the wind: and after the wind an earthquake; but the LORD was not in the earthquake: And after the earthquake a fire; but the LORD was not in the fire: and after the fire a still small voice. And it was so, when Elijah heard it, that he wrapped his face in his mantle, and went out, and stood in the entering in of the cave. And, behold, there came a voice unto him, and said, What doest thou here, Elijah? And he said, I have been very jealous for the LORD God of hosts: because the children of Israel have forsaken thy covenant, thrown down thine altars, and slain thy prophets with the sword; and I, even I only, am left; and they seek my life, to take it away. And the LORD said unto him, Go, return on thy way to the wilderness of Damascus: and when thou comest, anoint Hazael to be king over Syria: And Jehu the son of Nimshi shalt thou anoint to be king over Israel: and Elisha the son of Shaphat of Abelmeholah shalt thou anoint to be prophet in thy room. And it shall come to pass, that him that escapeth the sword of Hazael shall Jehu slay: and him that escapeth from the sword of Jehu shall Elisha slay. Yet I have left me seven thousand in Israel, all the knees which have not bowed unto Baal, and every mouth which hath not kissed him.

1 Kings 19:4–18 (KJV)

Elijah in his humanity was tired, hungry, and just plain worn out. He was spent on God's behalf and now needed to be filled again. He cried out for God to take his life, saying that he was no better than his fathers. Elijah lived zealously for God's words, to fulfill His purposes, but there is a reality to the physical state of our bodies affecting our mind and emotions.

The angel appeared to him, touched him, told him to eat and drink. He did and then lay down again. The angel touched him again and said, "Arise, eat, because the journey is too great for thee." The word of the Lord that he was receiving another assignment was enough to get him up. He went forty days and nights in the strength of that meat. The angel told him to eat, which he did, but that wasn't enough to revive him—he lay down again. It wasn't until the angel spoke again, this time adding that he needed to eat for the journey God was sending him on. It was the assignment that rejuvenated him and gave him purpose. After he heard that, he was able to get up again. How many times have we seen that in our lives? We go along, wounded, tired, and dry in spirit. Then we hear a word from the Lord, whether it be from His Word or from another believer, or from the Holy Spirit speaking in our circumstances. At the moment our spirit is touched, we are able to get up again. We are refreshed, revived, and ready to go forward once again. The Word of the Lord is meat for us; it sustains us until His purpose for that Word is accomplished. The Word of the Lord does not return void, but it accomplishes that for which it is purposed (Isa. 55:11). Seeing Him in our circumstances, recognizing that He is still with us and cares about us, this is what opens the eyes of our spirit and revives us; when we get a glimpse of His purpose. His sending sustains us. We can call to our remembrance the inner vision that we received in the enlightenment of the moment of His sending.

# Shocking: We Must "See" to "Be" and "Act" in Faith to Make It "Fact"

## ELISHA

And it came to pass, when the LORD would take up Elijah into heaven by a whirlwind, that Elijah went with Elisha from Gilgal. And Elijah said unto Elisha, Tarry here, I pray thee; for the LORD hath sent me to Bethel. And Elisha said unto him, As the LORD liveth, and as thy soul liveth, I will not leave thee. So they went down to Bethel. And the sons of the prophets that were at Bethel came forth to Elisha, and said unto him, Knowest thou that the LORD will take away thy master from thy head to day? And he said, Yea, I know it; hold ye your peace. And Elijah said unto him, Elisha, tarry here, I pray thee; for the LORD hath sent me to Jericho. And he said, As the LORD liveth, and as thy soul liveth, I will not leave thee. So they came to Jericho. And the sons of the prophets that were at Jericho came to Elisha, and said unto him, Knowest thou that the LORD will take away thy master from thy head to day? And he answered, Yea, I know it; hold ye your peace. And Elijah said unto him, Tarry, I pray thee, here; for the LORD hath sent me to Jordan. And he said, As the LORD liveth, and as thy soul liveth, I will not leave thee. And they two went on. And fifty men of the sons of the prophets went, and stood to view afar off: and they two stood by Jordan. And Elijah took his mantle, and wrapped it together, and smote the waters, and they were divided hither and thither, so that they two went over on dry ground. And it came to pass, when they were gone over, that Elijah said unto Elisha, Ask what I shall do for thee, before I be taken away from thee. And Elisha said, I pray thee, let a double portion of thy spirit be upon me. And he said, Thou hast asked a hard thing: nevertheless, if thou see me when I am taken from thee, it shall be so unto thee; but if not, it shall not be so. And it came to pass, as they still went on, and talked, that, behold, there appeared a chariot of fire, and horses of fire, and parted them both asunder; and Elijah went up by a whirlwind into heaven. And Elisha saw it, and he cried, My father, my father, the chariot of Israel, and the horsemen thereof. And he saw him no more: and he took hold of his own clothes, and rent them in two pieces. He took up also the mantle of Elijah that fell from him, and went back, and stood by the bank of Jordan; And he took the mantle of Elijah that fell from him, and smote the waters, and said, Where is the LORD God of Elijah? and when he also had smitten the waters, they parted hither and thither: and Elisha went over. And when the sons of the prophets which were to view at Jericho saw him, they said, The spirit of Elijah doth rest on Elisha. And they came to meet him, and bowed themselves to the ground before him.

2 Kings 2:1–15 (KJV)

Why did Elijah tell Elisha to tarry and not to follow? To tarry means to sit down, to dwell, to remain, to settle and ease self. I believe that Elijah was testing Elisha to see if he truly desired to follow, because to walk in the high things of God requires persistence and pressing on to new levels. There is a testing of faith versus presumption. God may bring people into your life who speak the opposite of what He has said, who seem adverse to you, to get you to speak your destiny forth. Note that Elisha said, "As the Lord liveth, and as my soul liveth, I will not leave thee." He knew what it would take to live in the spirit, and he was determined to have it.

Elisha asked for a double portion of Elijah's spirit when Elijah was to be taken up. Elijah said it was a hard thing to ask for, but "if thou see me taken from thee, it shall be so unto thee; if not, it shall not be so." Elijah knew that in order to walk in that level of spiritual anointing and authority, you have to be able to see with spiritual eyes. Elisha saw, believed, and walked in faith, taking an immediate action, rending his clothes in two pieces (representing the double portion he believed for), taking the mantle of Elijah and smiting the waters of Jordan, declaring "where is the God of Elijah" and the water parted.

How often do we see, and believe, and confess the word of the Lord to us, then do not take the corresponding step of faith? Immediately doubt will set in if you don't take a step of faith. The opportunity arises; if we hesitate, our minds will begin to reason and doubt. Faith is not faith if it is something we can see in the natural; no faith is required, the thing is obviously there. His supernatural power comes as we obey. The word itself enables belief (faith comes by hearing and hearing by the word of God—Rom. 10:17); we must will to do His will, yield our bodies as a living sacrifice to Him and do something. Faith without works is dead (James 2:17–26). It is God Himself who works in us to cause us to will and do of His pleasure (Phil. 2:13), yet our flesh is ever present, warring against the Spirit of God (Rom. 8).

We need persistence to press into what God has spoken over our lives. There will always be a temptation to settle. In this account, we see that there are three levels of persistence that I believe are common to all Christians—Bethel, Jericho, and Jordan. Bethel means house of God; Jericho means city of palm trees, a fragrant and refreshing place, a place where fruit is borne; Jordan means flowing down, or symbolic of descending, dying to self.

Bethel is significant in our lives in recognizing the heavenly and spiritual aspects of faith—realizing that everything comes from God. He is present in our lives, and we must believe in Him and trust in Him. Once we begin to walk with Him in faith and obedience, there will be fruit produced—the fragrance of Christ that is released—this is our Jericho. Then we enter into the refinement process, our Jordan, where we must die to self. Here even the gifts, the good things that God has released into our lives, must be given back to Him so that He can trust us with intimacy. This is the place where ego is left behind, where only the presence of God matters, not doing for Him but being one with Him.

## Shocking: For Success in His Kingdom, We Need Revelation, Not Information

### REVELATION BRINGS IMPARTATION TO CARRY US TO HIS DESTINATION

> And it came to pass, when Joshua was by Jericho, that he lifted up his eyes and looked, and, behold, there stood a man over against him with his sword drawn in his hand: and Joshua went unto him, and said unto him, Art thou for us, or for our adversaries? And he said, Nay; but as captain of the host of the LORD am I now come. And Joshua fell on his face to the earth, and did worship, and said unto him, What saith my LORD unto his servant? And the captain of the LORD's host said unto Joshua, Loose thy shoe from off thy foot; for the place whereon thou standest is holy. And Joshua did so.
>
> Joshua 5:13–15 (KJV)

Joshua received revelation of Jesus as captain of the Host of the Lord. It is important to see that the Lord's army is not sent to be for or against a people, but to represent the Lord and fulfill His will. God is for us to the extent that we are for Him. If we are against Him, He will be against us. He cannot be unfaithful to His purposes. He has given His word and will perform it. His creative force, all His resources are for His purposes. We choose this day whom we will serve; if God, it must be from a place of worship, for He is Holy and where He is, is Holy ground.

On Holy ground he is told to loose his shoe (as with Moses, Ex. 3:5). Shoes are symbolic of where we walk in the world. God told Moses, "I am that I am," or, "I will be what you need me to be when you need me to be it." In Moses's case, God was revealed as the deliverer of Moses when he was a baby, and then Moses was to become deliverer of the Hebrew people. The revelation of Jesus as captain of the Lord of Hosts was necessary for Joshua to have faith to go forward as captain and lead the people into the Promised Land. To take Jericho, Joshua would need supernatural means, supernatural vision to see the provision and believe it. His eyes were opened to the reality of the Host of the Lord led by the Divine Captain.

If God is calling you to do a new thing, or if you are in a trial where there is no way you can succeed on your natural abilities, you will need a new revelation of who He is. God desires to prosper us to bring His kingdom; we must seek Him in the trial of our faith until we receive the revelation of who He is that will bring the promise to fruition.

Consider this, If He is in us, then where we go, He goes; therefore, wherever we go is holy ground and set apart for His purposes. My God and My Lord, if we were to really believe this, what would be accomplished in this world! Of course, we have to be sure that we are not tempting God by putting ourselves in a place that He hasn't told us to be. Remember that Satan tempted Jesus to jump off the cliff, quoting scripture that God would give His angels charge over him. Jesus knew that God hadn't told him to do that but that Satan was trying to get him out of the will of God. If God has called you to a thing, Satan will try to tempt you out of it and may even use scripture to justify it or a Christian to deliver it. Remember, Satan used Peter to try and get Jesus out of the will of God, and Jesus said to Peter, "Get thee behind me, Satan" (Matt. 16:22–23) God's leading will never go against His Word, but people can take scriptures out of context to justify following their own desires.

## Shocking: The Eyes of Your Heart Determine Your Perception

### WHO DOES YOUR HEART ENTRUST ITSELF TO—GOD, YOURSELF, OR SOMEONE ELSE?

In 2 Chronicles 16:9 (NKJV), we read, "For the eyes of Jehovah run to and fro in all the whole earth to show Himself strong on behalf of those whose heart is perfect toward Him." A perfect heart concerning God is complete and undivided; one that is not perceiving Him to be evil, unjust, unrighteous, unloving. A perfect heart recognizes that He is perfect; there is no unrighteousness in Him, and He is worthy of all of our devotion and love. A perfect heart is one of full trusting obedience, only wanting to be with Him.

> Therefore thus says the Lord [to Jeremiah]: If you return [and give up this mistaken tone of distrust and despair], then I will give you again a settled place of quiet and safety, and you will be My minister; and if you separate the precious from the vile [cleansing your own heart from unworthy and unwarranted suspicions concerning God's faithfulness], you shall be My mouthpiece. [But do not yield to them.] Let them return to you—not you to [the people]. And I will make you to this people a fortified, bronze wall; they will fight against you, but they will not prevail over you, for I am with you to save and deliver you, says the Lord. And I will deliver you out of the hands of the wicked, and I will redeem you out of the palms of the terrible and ruthless tyrants.
>
> Jeremiah 15:19–21 (Amplified)

Thus saith the LORD; Cursed be the man that trusteth in man, and maketh flesh his arm, and whose heart departeth from the LORD. For he shall be like the heath in the desert, and shall not see when good cometh; but shall inhabit the parched places in the wilderness, in a salt land and not inhabited. Blessed is the man that trusteth in the LORD, and whose hope the LORD is. For he shall be as a tree planted by the waters, and that spreadeth out her roots by the river, and shall not see when heat cometh, but her leaf shall be green; and shall not be careful in the year of drought, neither shall cease from yielding fruit. The heart is deceitful above all things, and desperately wicked: who can know it? I the LORD search the heart, I try the reins, even to give every man according to his ways, and according to the fruit of his doings.

Jeremiah 17:5–10 (KJV)

The heart directs our seeing; the heart that trusts God will open our eyes to see goodness, abundance, and growth. If our heart doesn't trust God, we see lack, desolation, and drought.

God wants to show Himself strong on our behalf—if we would but trust Him and His goodness!

It is foolish to trust man—man represents the flesh and the natural. God, who created us and to whom we will return, is the only one that is completely trustworthy and the one who creates our circumstances, who has the supernatural ability to transform and create. Remember, Jesus entrusted Himself to no man, for He knew what was in them (John 2:24). We are told to examine ourselves, to determine whether we are in the faith or not (2 Cor. 13:5). If not, we need to remind ourselves of who He is, what He has done and will continue to do. Our eyes will be opened and we will see His provision, His strength, and delivering power.

# SHOCKING: THE REALITY THAT HIS PURPOSE FOR OUR LIVES IS TO BRING HIS KINGDOM TO THE EARTH

## Shocking: There Is a God-given Destiny for Our Lives, and Circumstances Are Ordained to That End

### MOSES

Moses was divinely chosen to be the deliverer. His very birth speaks of deliverance: from Pharaoh's edict that all baby boys would die, he was delivered into Pharaoh's own house. He would later come back to Pharaoh to ask for deliverance for his people. He would then be in a position where he was known. God was preparing him for his future position. Moses knew the ways of the Egyptians yet was a Hebrew by birth. Truly, who you are, the purpose and destiny God has planned for you, will be brought forth by divine direction. There are no accidents in your circumstances. What you go through will be necessary for your future as purposed by God. We still have a choice. Moses, when God spoke to Him, did not have to do it. He could have said no. In fact, he was reluctant because of his own insecurities and ended up having his brother do the actual speaking. He was more comfortable in the role of intermediary. Regardless, he is the one God chose to speak to directly.

The Bible says Moses was very meek, more than all the others on the face of the earth (Num. 12:3).

In this instance, meek, according to Strong's Concordance, means depressed figuratively; in mind gentle or circumstances

needy or saintly; humble, lowly, poor.[45] Depressed in Webster's
Dictionary means lacking energy or enthusiasm; melancholy,
gloomy.[46] This is the man God chose to lead the people out of
bondage? He was the perfect candidate because he knew he had
nothing within himself to give and had to completely rely upon
God! This meekness was not innate—this meekness was borne
in him from his experiences, having been broken by the actions
of his pride, the consequences of his sin. Remember, he had been
born a deliverer and set about to do so in his own strength; full
of pride, acting out of his emotions, he killed a man. This caused
him to flee into the desert, where he learned patience, humility,
and dependence on God's voice and direction. His desert experience also gave him the ability to understand the people's experience in their desert as they wandered through the wilderness on
route to the Promised Land. Moses was an archetype of Jesus, as
mediator between God and man, and as deliverer out of bondage.

# JOSEPH

Joseph's life is one of the best examples of circumstances in life
being orchestrated to further God's purposes. He had the favor
of God on his life—for a purpose. He had two prophetic dreams
that indicated he would rule over his brothers and even his father
and mother. He was his father's favorite son. This caused his
brothers to be intensely jealous, so much so that they left him in
a pit to die, then one of the brothers had an attack of conscience
and convinced them it would be better to sell Joseph into slavery.

Joseph was then taken into Potiphar's house as a slave. Potiphar
was one of Pharaoh's officials, captain of the palace guard. Joseph
found favor with Potiphar, and Potiphar placed him in charge of
the whole household. Potiphar's wife then tries to seduce him.
When he wouldn't go along with it because it would be a sin
against Potiphar as well as God, she told everyone he raped her,
and he was thrown into prison.

Now in prison, Joseph once again found favor. Through God giving him discernment to interpret dreams, he ended up in the palace. Through the favor of God on his life, he was able to warn Pharaoh about an impending seven-year famine and to provide a God-given strategy on how to get through the famine. Subsequently, Joseph was once again raised up by the favor of God, as governor of Egypt.

Joseph's brothers came to Egypt for food during the seven-year famine, and God was able to bring reconciliation to the family. This wasn't the full story, though. God used this famine to bring Israel to Egypt, the next step in His plan. Joseph recognized God's sovereignty even in all that he had been through and was able to say to his brothers, "You intended to harm me, but God intended it for good to accomplish what is now being done, the saving of many lives" (Gen. 50:20).

Through all these events of Joseph's life, God was working for the good of Joseph and the whole of Israel. Joseph knew that, and that's why he persevered and received God's favor, even in the midst of terrible afflictions and trials. I can't help but think that Joseph had faith because of those prophetic dreams and held on to them in his heart when he was tested and tried so many times. Joseph's life prefigured Jesus's life—he was loved by his father and hated by his brothers, the word given (Joseph's dreams, Jesus's experience at His baptism) tested three times, both thirty years old when they came into their ministry; faithful through sufferings and raised to authority.

# JESUS

Jesus was sent into the wilderness by the Holy Spirit where he was tempted by Satan for forty days and nights. He knows our temptations, having been tempted in all things as we are. Through his death, resurrection, and ascension, the Holy Spirit has now been poured out. We who believe in him have allowed our old man to die with him and received his life, so that we can all hear

God and be led by Him into His purposes and the fulfillment of our destiny in Christ Jesus. Trust God in your circumstances, regardless of what they look like in the natural, knowing that He is sovereign and what you see right now is not the end of the story. He is working on your behalf! Praise Him in the midst of all of your trials and you will see His favor on your life!

## Shocking: God's Tests Are Meant to Result in Kingdom Manifestation in Our Lives

After deliverance from Egypt and crossing the sea, following with exuberant praise and worship, they were three days in the wilderness with no water (Exodus 15). Then they came to a place of water, and it was bitter (I wonder if the water was bitter all along or only after they stopped praising). The people murmured against Moses, and he cried unto the Lord. The Lord showed him a tree, which when Moses cast it into the waters, the waters were made sweet: there He made for them a statute and an ordinance, and there He proved them (testing).

- First test—Will you believe I am good, that I am here, that I am leading you, even if the circumstances don't look like it?

- Second test–Will you believe my word, that I am faithful and can be trusted to bring it to pass? My words do not fail; they accomplish that for which they are purposed.

- Third test—Will you continue to praise Me when your life doesn't look like you think it should, when the feelings of delight and exuberance in your blessings are gone?

- Fourth test–Will you come to Me when you are discouraged, bringing Me your concerns and fears? Cry unto Me and I will answer...I will make the bitter waters of life sweet.

- Fifth test—Will you, in faith, take the action that is required? Will you do what I have commanded? My ways may seem strange until you obey, then you see.

It was there, at the bitter waters made sweet, that He made for them a statute (an enactment, an appointment) and an ordinance (a verdict, a formal decree). He showed Moses a tree, which represents the cross—Christ taking on our suffering and sin for which only atonement, innocent blood, is the answer. The atoning work of Christ on the cross brings fresh, sweet life-giving water to every bitter experience that we cannot handle.

Believe in Him. He makes our bitter waters sweet. He brings victory and increase when we believe. The circumstances may look bad, bringing an opportunity to believe, and God makes it better; or we murmur in unbelief, making it bitter.

God brought them to a place, again, of dependence and trust. He then taught them, for they were in a place of open ears and hearts. He said,

> And said, If thou wilt diligently hearken to the voice of the LORD thy God, and wilt do that which is right in his sight, and wilt give ear to his commandments, and keep all his statutes, I will put none of these diseases upon thee, which I have brought upon the Egyptians: for I am the LORD that healeth thee.
>
> Exodus 15:26 (KJV)

According to Strong's Concordance, keep in this instance means to adhere to, to become one with.[47] We have to recognize everything in us that does not agree or conform to His Word and bring it to the cross. Let God be true and every man a liar. He is true, but in our lives we have to let Him show Himself as true. When we keep His word and trust our circumstances to Him, He proves Himself. This is "letting" Him be seen as true.

> For what if some did not believe? shall their unbelief make the faith of God without effect? God forbid: yea, let God be true, but every man a liar; as it is written, That thou mightest be justified in thy sayings, and mightest overcome when thou art judged.
>
> Romans 3:3–4 (KJV)

The end result of taking every thought captive to the obedience of Christ is that you will receive grace as Christ is revealed (1 Pet. 1:13). Yes, on that final day, but in the present day, there is judgment for our words and actions; there are present consequences. It isn't a punishment, but rather it is fruit being reaped for what we have sown. Each moment is an opportunity to live in the spirit or the flesh; what we sow reaps a harvest.

After teaching and testing, and passing the tests, He brought them to Elim (meaning oaks) where there were twelve wells of water (twelve tribes, twelve apostles; 12 is a symbol of divine government) and seventy palm trees (70 is the number of increase: Jesus sent out the twelve, then the seventy). If faithful, God will bring us to a place of order and increase. Palm trees are a symbol of victory. They encamped there by the waters.

## ORDER OF CHRISTIAN EXPERIENCE

After death to self/desires, there comes a testing period to see if we are faithful to what was taught (three days with no water is symbolic of the grave—dying to self). If we endure, we allow His divine government to take place in and through us and we receive the life of Christ (tree) in this situation—increase and victory. He brings new revelation of who He is, His purposes, and our position.

I believe that in this hour of the body of Christ, there is a sifting, as God tests our faith, individually and corporately, while we move into the new wineskin. The sifting must come, that His purposes remain. The old religious mindset, of traditions and systems built so that we can understand and predict and control outcomes (or so we think), must be set aside so that the Spirit of God can direct in accordance with His will.

He is repositioning the church, establishing His apostolic government so that we can operate in His divine authority and bring increase of His government and kingdom in the earth today. His word says that this is the order, that through the gifts of apostle, prophet, evangelist, pastor, and teacher, the body of Christ will be equipped for the work of the ministry. It must be in place, all members of the body working together in their gifts and callings, so that we can manifest to the principalities and powers the manifold wisdom of God through the church!

## *Shocking: God Will Cause Time to Stand Still to Accomplish His Purposes*

> Joshua commanded the sun and moon to stand still; the sun at Gibeon and the moon in the valley of Ajabon; until the people had avenged themselves on their enemies. And there was no day like that before it or after it, where the LORD hearkened unto the voice of a man: for the LORD fought for Israel.
>
> Joshua 10:12–14 (KJV)

God gives us creative power in our words and had given Joshua authority as a leader of the people. Moses was supposed to have walked in this authority; he was given the opportunity at the rock but allowed his flesh to rule.

God desires that we be in such a place of oneness with Him that our words are His words of authority—to accomplish His purposes. We can't be if we are in covenant with the world.

1 Samuel 3:19 says of the prophet Samuel that not one of his words fell to the ground. He spoke what God said. God will fulfill His word; not one will return to Him void of His purpose being brought forth (Isaiah 55:11) .

God will cause time to stand still to accomplish His purposes—to deliver from the enemy and bring victory, His kingdom to come on this earth. Remember, one day with the Lord is as one thousand years (2 Peter 3:8). Time is eternal with God; there is no beginning or end. Time was created so that we may measure our days and accomplish the tasks that will establish His kingdom on earth. When we are rightly aligned to His purposes, He will move heaven and earth to accomplish them. Your perception of your past, all the mistakes you have made, will be opened as He shifts things into His alignment and you will see that He worked it all to His end and your good.

I have seen that it is a steadfast principle that when I place God first in my life, He blesses the rest of my time, and in effect, my time seems to be increased. I am able to accomplish more in a shorter amount of time. It is the same principle as first fruits; when you give God the first, the rest is blessed.

We don't know how He caused time to stand still in this account. We do know that He created time, He created the sun and the moon, and all things created by Him are subject to Him and to His voice. Jesus stilled the wind and the waves. He said we can move mountains by speaking to them. Elijah spoke that God would do a new thing and the earth would open up and destroy the prophets of Baal. This happened. God caused the Red Sea to part so the Israelites could escape the Egyptians. If you are abiding in the realm of eternity, that is, in His presence doing His work, should time have an effect? I have not experienced it, but I know people who have been interceding and were transported to another locale and much took place for the kingdom. When they returned, little time had passed. Did time stand still? We don't know. I, for one, choose to believe that with God, all things are possible. He is Lord of all.

## *Shocking: His Purpose Encompasses His Love; His Love Brings You into His Purpose*

"And He brought us out from there so that He might bring us in to give us the land which He swore to our fathers" (Deut. 6:23 NKJV). He brought us out to bring us in! His purpose is even greater than His love for us. You might think He brought you out, delivered you, because He loves you, and oh how He does love you. But He brought you out so that He could bring you in; in to His greater purposes, in to His Kingdom, in to blessing upon blessing and increase upon increase; so that He could be manifested in and through you and bring others in. Your testimony of His goodness and greatness is needed in this world. The world testifies of sickness, loss, and destruction. The life of Christ in you testifies to abundance in every realm.

His purpose is greater than His love; it encompasses His love for us. His purpose is reconciliation of all things to Himself—He is love; reconciled to love is His purpose. His purpose is love; love is His purpose.

"But I say to you that Elijah has come already, and they did not know him, but have done to him whatever they desired. Likewise also the Son of Man shall suffer from them" (Matt. 17:12 NKJV). God will not save us from suffering; it is part of His plan to fulfill His purposes. Others' salvation may come through our suffering; godly character is built as we suffer in the flesh.

This is an example of how His purpose is greater than His love for the individual. The greater purpose encompasses His love—as we understand love. We expect love will want to save us from suffering. Yet that very suffering, in the flesh, may be the thing that will shame others into seeking God, or into a place where they can hear, or be a memory they will retrieve later. Also, our suffering in the flesh allows the life of Christ (His Spirit) to be stronger in us. As we die, He lives. The flesh wars against the Spirit; the flesh is enmity against God (Rom. 8:7, Gal. 5:16–17).

"But the God of all grace, who hath called us unto his eternal glory by Christ Jesus, after that ye have suffered a while, make you perfect, stablish, strengthen, settle you" (1 Pet. 5:10 KJV). We are perfected through our suffering. In the grand scheme of God's purposes, our suffering creates in us godly character—faithfulness to Him no matter what, and His glory revealed through us. Steven was stoned for preaching the Word of God. As he was stoned, He saw Jesus, and others saw Jesus through him. Jesus suffered and rose three days later. And having His many sufferings at our hands, He remained faithful and true, and was empowered by God and ministered to by angels. Many sons were brought, and are being brought, unto glory.

This is His purpose; this is His love. In John 17, Jesus prayed we would be one with the Father and receive the same glory He has. Greater suffering in the flesh brings us into a greater realm of glory as He fills that place in us with His glory! This is His purpose, to be filled with His glory and let His glory cover the earth, restoring His kingdom! It is time to arise and shine, letting the light of His glory fill us and move through us. It is time to declare that His glory fills the earth as the waters cover the sea. It is time to speak forth the truth and see it manifest in the earth as we declare the goodness of God and the lordship of Jesus Christ. It is time to speak words of life to the dead so that those dead bones will rise and become a mighty army of the Living God! Arise! Shine!

# ENDNOTES

1    James Strong, New Strong's Concordance of the Bible (Nashville: Thomas Nelson, 1995) s.v. "Omri."

2    Strong, s.v. "vanities."

3    Merriam Webster's Collegiate Dictionary, Tenth Edition (Philippines: 1994) , s.v. "vanity.'

4    Webster, s.v. vain.

5    Strong, s.v. Levi.

6    Strong, s.v. calves.

7    Strong, s.v. reproach.

8    Strong, s.v. knowledge.

9    Strong, s.v. subtil.

10    Strong, s.v. issues.

11    Strong, s.v. vain.

12    Strong, s.v. drought.

13    Strong, s.v. Ramah.

14    Strong, s.v. meditate.

15    Strong, s.v. wear out.

16    Strong, s.v. heard.

17    Strong, s.v. enchantments.

18    Webster, s.v. prognosticate.

19    Strong, s.v. Baal-Peor.

20    Strong, s.v. anger.

21    Strong, s.v. snare.

22    Webster, s.v. snare.

23    Strong, s.v. traps.

24    Webster, s.v. goad.

25    Strong, s.v. thorns.

26    Strong, s.v. gainsaying.

27    Strong, s.v. abide.

28    Strong, s.v. promised.

29    Strong, s.v. cleft.

30    Strong, s.v. discourage.

31    Strong, s.v. loatheth.

32    Strong, s.v. chide.

33    Strong, s.v. err.

34    Strong, s.v. evil and slander.

35    Strong, s.v. slander.

36    Strong, s.v. faithful.

37    Strong, s.v. line.

38    Strong, s.v. redemption.

39    Strong, s.v. body.

40    Strong, s.v. similitude.

41    Strong, s.v. distil.

42    Strong, s.v. dew.

43    Strong, s.v. rain.

44    Strong, s.v. showers.

45    Strong, s.v. meek.

46    Webster, s.v. depressed.

47    Strong, s.v. keep.